The House In The Faythe

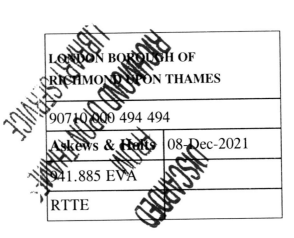

The House in the Faythe

Vonnie Banville Evans

WEXFORD

Code Green Publishing

First published in Ireland
by Poolbeg Press Ltd. in 1994.
This edition by Code Green Publishing 2010

ISBN 978-1-907215-13-1

Version 1.0

Cover design by Barry Evans
Illustrations by Vonnie Banville Evans

Published by
Code Green Publishing
Coventry, England
www.codegreenpublishing.com

For my family and friends, then and now

Contents

Chapter 1: The House in the Faythe

I can't say I remember "the house where I was born", but I can say I remember the house where I came to life. As a matter of fact, my very first memory is of walking, hand in hand, with my father across the Faythe from Castle Hill Street in a diagonal line to Swan View. My father had a most distinctive walk. He sort of tapped one foot, the left one, off the ground, like someone starting off a hornpipe. As a child I always knew his walk before he came into sight. My mother always insisted that I was raving. I could not possibly remember that first entry into the house in the Faythe as I was all of two years of age when we moved there. But I do remember. As I said, it was the beginning for me:

"In the beginning she walked across the Faythe and entered the house with her father."

I have started in my mind, many months ago, to write this down and maybe the digging has laid bare many things I had forgotten in my adult years. Mostly the great love I had for my father when I was a very young child. I think my father was a tremendously kind man before living managed to confuse him. That day must have been one of his first times in the house because he went through it and up to the attic. The attic was to become a great place of mystery to me as a child and I often suspect that many of my dreams now are based there or centre around it. I know as I grow older, instead of diminishing, my thoughts about that house, and my childhood there, take on an even more magical quality.

I can remember only good times, and great deep swellings of happiness. So much so that I am constantly amazed myself by the richness my memory throws up.

My father helped me up the wooden stairway and into the attic. It was brown, a lovely dark brown feeling, and the floor was covered by layers and layers of newspaper. My father had to take a shovel to them to remove some of the layers. I have no memory of dust, dirt or cobwebs. Maybe these things don't exist for a two-year-old. The experts could probably tell me how much it is possible to be aware of at that tender age.

Well I can close my eyes now and be aware again of the warmth of that dark brown place, with the newspaper layer carpet and the strong arms of my father as he dug at it with his shovel. I can sense his happiness. He must have been looking forward to living in this house and maybe that is why I came to love it so much. I know he did not want to leave it when the time eventually came.

I believe, deep down in my melodramatic soul, that he was broken-hearted when we did leave. In some strange way he gave up living his life – left it locked away in Swan View, with my youth and a happiness I could never quite recapture.

Happy memories come tumbling out. Could it really have been so wonderful? Is this why life has always seemed an anticlimax since those early days in the Faythe? Or is this how we all remember as we grow old? Do we delete everything we want to forget and only add more vibrancy to the colours of the joy, laying it on with a palette-knife. thicker and thicker every day, or every time we allow ourselves to remember?

My life then was the family. My prayer, "God Bless Mammy and Daddy, Vincent and Jack and all my relations and friends," still comes first from the subconscious whenever I kneel at my bed with a tired mind. The house itself was built solidly of stone with the front door opening straight on to the street. It had a hallway running straight through from front to back. About three-quarters-way down the hall hung a green curtain which was tied back to the side. The floor covering was a sort of beige lino which my mother scrubbed every Saturday. I used to take the straw mats, round and made by the lightship men, out into the street and bang them off the cement path. There they lay until the hall was dry and then they were lovingly replaced until the following week. The Room, with capital letters, was on the right-hand side. It would, in our anglicised or Americanised modern times, be referred to as the lounge-cum-dining-room. To us it was The Room, pure and simple.

It too ran from the front window, scene of my brother Jack's mysterious accident which turned him into a kitogue, to the back window looking out into the yard. Jack entered the window alcove one day, right-handed like all good children. He emerged shortly afterwards holding a wounded right hand up under his jacket and began to use his left hand much to my mother's annoyance. The good nuns in the babies' class threatened and cajoled and eventually slapped. It was all to no avail. Jack was adamant and proceeded to use the left hand to eat and eventually to write. But he had the last laugh over mother and nuns for he became ambidextrous and could switch from one hand to the other with ease.

Under the window in the back wall stood a folding card-chair, never folded. Beside this chair, inside a little door, was the gas meter, a thing of wonder which gave off a strange smell and swallowed shillings. It ensured that we had light at night. No electricity in those days, just two globes in the wall at each side of the range. These were ceremoniously lit every evening, the curtains drawn and the world settled down at our fire side, mellow and well-rounded and totally at peace. Ah, those nights around the range in The Room. I remember the little wooden chair with the hole in each arm where a wooden baton could be inserted to keep a child firmly in place. I never suffered the indignity of being imprisoned by the piece of wood but I sat in that chair, in front of the glowing fire, which was safely enclosed behind bars in the black range. My mother spent much of her time rubbing at this range with black lead until it shone. Here also was the scene of one of my first moments of real terror, the day I chased my little brother across the polished hall from the scullery only to see him trip and hit his head off the bars of the, mercifully unlit, range. I am sure he bears the scar to this day. I wonder does he remember that fall and the ensuing hubbub and the trouble I was in for being the cause of his downfall. But then I was usually the cause of any calamity that befell us. I suppose that was the way in most Irish homes then, where the family consisted of one girl and two boys!

On the left of the hall was the parlour which remained for most of my childhood the "glory hole."

Things were kept there, including my young brother when he was a baby. He slept in a big, low-slung, grey pram. That is, when he slept and that was not often and not for long. I believe the reason my blood runs cold, even to this day, when I hear a baby crying, has nothing to do with the babyhood of my own three sons (the youngest one turned out to be just as miserly about the amount of time he allowed for sleep in the first few years of his life). It goes back down the tunnels of my mind, to the time when my older brother and myself woke the baby from his precious slumber, and his wail rang out, bringing my mother running swiftly (we both got a slap in the ear as she passed on her way) to try to coax him back to sleep, something she knew could take up the best part of her morning, or prove impossible.

How can I move on here without telling of the awful day the pram ran away on me with Jack inside? I was accused of trying to kill him. This may indeed have been the beginning of the legend which grew up in my life story, that I was in some way a dark person, peculiar and maybe even a bit mad. My mother never trusted my father's family and made vague references to their precarious states of mind. On one occasion, in the middle of one of the fierce rows that always blazed out between us, she told me in a sad voice that she could not understand me and that I was a bit touched. My rows with my mother were always there between us like a smouldering fire waiting for a breeze to bring it to life and believe me I had a windy childhood. This did not worry me unduly because I knew quite well how impossible it was for anyone to understand me, especially my mother. She seemed so far outside my world of happiness. She worried about money and other silly things like most other adults and she did not devote her every conscious minute to enjoying and exploring the wonder of being alive.

Anyhow on the fateful day my mother put the baby into the big pram and we headed off down the street to visit my aunt who lived just across on the other side. I begged to be let push the pram up and down while she was inside enjoying the visit. Against her better judgement, and after issuing many threats about what would happen if anything happened she allowed me to take charge. I pushed importantly up and down the path being extremely careful.

As with everything in life, I soon became ambitious and felt confident enough to go further afield. Now just up the path was a rise which was quite steep and off I went. By dint of much effort I got the pram up to the top of the rise. I was about five years old and a very small person, so of course the inevitable happened. The pram ran away and the baby ended up out on the path. I remember my feeling of sheer horror and mind-bending panic. Of course, life being what it is, the usually wailing boy was silent, making us all think he was badly injured, maybe even dead. My mother and my aunt came running and the rest is a blur in my mind. I do remember the feeling of total injustice, though I could not have put a name on it at the time. This was my first brush with something that becomes so familiar in all our lives. Words like jealous were bandied about and the implication that I had done it on purpose, in order to get rid of the opposition, hung in the air. How could they think that, when I loved the baby so much and had been so careful? How wrong adults can be and how they damage children by thinking they are capable of large evil when they really are not.

Back to the description of the house. Across the hall from the Room was the scullery which was fairly primitive even in those days. It possessed a sink with one cold tap and an ancient gas cooker. Outside the scullery was the stairs which were dark and winding, and which I loved. I wonder why I had such an affinity for dark places as a child? Aren't children supposed to be afraid of the dark?

What does it say about me that I had no fear of the dark until I became an adult?

At the top of the stairs was the first bedroom which was never used, except for one brief time when my grandfather came to live with us. I often wondered about this room and I learned in later years that my mother believed it to be haunted. This was very peculiar because my mother was a most practical woman, not given to flights of fancy. In fact, she was the strong one in the partnership and the one who took more and more control of everything as time went on, until my father became more of a disinterested onlooker than a participant in life.

The story as I had it from my mother's own lips, was that she had many sightings of a girl or woman in the doorway of that room and she became terrified of the stairs and of the house itself. I suspect that this is why she campaigned so vehemently to leave it and get a new house. She told me once that she recounted the story of the ghost to a woman she knew and when this woman asked her to describe the vision she gave an accurate description of a young woman who had lived and died in our house. She died of the dreaded TB and in the very room at the top of the stairs. The family were distantly related to this woman my mother confided in. As my mother was born and reared in the neighbouring town of Enniscorthy she had no knowledge of the house or its occupants before we moved in.

This was my mother's story and I believed her. She was not given to telling yarns or exaggerating. We children were forbidden to go up or down the stairs alone because it was dangerous. I remember once asking my father what was wrong, sensing an atmosphere of something amiss. He told me there was a rat in the coal hole under the stairs and this satisfied me. There was always a statue of the Blessed Virgin in that room, so my mother was obviously taking no chances. None of this bothered me, nor did it affect my love for the house in the Faythe.

Chapter 2: The Attic

I think I actually went into the attic only once more in my life. I know I have a vague memory of potatoes spread on the floor, so it must have been winter, and looking out through a little window down over the gardens and up to Pat Molloy's field and the Rocks beyond. We were forbidden to go up there, maybe the floor was not safe to walk on or, maybe, it too had its ghost. However, for some reason, probably the very fact that it was a forbidden place, the attic became for me the entry into another world. I never knew, until my sons discovered and introduced me to the Narnia books, that CS Lewis had been there before me and I to certainly would not like to try explain the psychology behind it, but the three steps up and the brown door through which I was never again to enter became the opening into a wonderful world where I was the power that was!

I suppose all children live in their own world or certainly their own idea of the world and maybe the more imaginative ones make this as real as the one they physically inhabit. So it was with me. I was never a very robust child and I spent long days in my sick-bed or in my case on my sick-couch. No chaise-longue for me but a wooden couch in the corner of the room – just a little more modern than the "settle" found in most country cottages of the time. This couch, for want of a better word, was attached to the wall at the far end of the room. It was, as I said, made of wood and had a carved end with a press underneath which was in effect a glory hole containing all sorts of rubbish together with more legitimate shoe polish, brushes, dusters, etc. As we got older and amassed possessions of our own, my brothers and I kept our boxes in this press, so it became very special to us.

I suffered all the known childhood illnesses and a special one of my own. This mysterious sickness came in the form of a raging headache and sick stomach which laid me low for two or three days of intense agony. Usually on the third day I would be gloriously sick and the recovery would be almost as instantaneous as the onset of the attack. Still ensconced on my bed of pain I would be treated royally by my father who produced tea and toast, the first food and drink to be consumed since the pangs in my head began three days before. No food or drink ever tasted as good as that tea and toast, except maybe the rasher and egg I was given the morning after my eldest son was born. At such times food takes on a mystical element or maybe it is that having suffered and been deprived, we see food for what it really is and understand that it is our life's strength.

This illness was referred to at the time as "bilious attacks." The more modern term, I suppose, would be migraine. For the duration of the headache I don't think I did any more than try to survive – I know I often banged my head off the wall and endured as near a state of despair as a young child can reach. But in the euphoric few days of recovery, when one was left to one's own devices by pain and parents alike, that same head which had suffered such indignity seemed to be set free from normal events and could and would soar up to the attic, out through the window, out over Pat Molloy's field and into a realm where living was all bliss.

In this nameless land I set about reliving my life the right way round. I could choose my own name, my appearance; the appearance of everything and everyone and the happenings were all controlled by me. This I did in a most meticulous way often spending days reliving events, changing the scenario over and over again until it suited my imagination which was rich in detail and very hard to please.

Since. the sea was my delight, it figured hugely in the attic land. It was there, vast and blue and tide-less, right outside the door of the house in the Faythe. I just had to step outside and into it and it rolled between our house and Tommy Kelly's pub across the street. It was always just the right depth and temperature for swimming. And I could swim like a fish, or better still, like Esther Williams, whom I had seen in a Saturday matinee.

So here I swam with the sun beating down and the palm trees swaying on the golden-sanded beaches. Here I could return whenever I liked, because once my scenes were set nobody but myself could interfere or change them. In this magical land I was the brightest, the bravest, the cleverest, the Boss, and there was no such thing as bilious attacks, toothache, earache or any ache. Here I had all the possessions I envied. Dolls that walked and talked, the cleverest animals, and a horse that I could ride bareback. I was a circus owner, a shopkeeper, but most of all, a darling child, adored by everyone – probably tall and blonde and elegant – not small and dark and troublesome. My parents were rich and beautiful and my brothers did what I told them to without question.

Every book I read I relived my way, and I was a voracious reader from the time I managed to make my way through Black Beauty at the age of five. I know I carried that book around under my arm for a very long time and I can still close my eyes and recall the feeling of amazed wonder I felt every time I opened it. Maybe that explains in some way the love I still have for books, not just in reading them, but books, the inanimate objects.

Every film I was lucky enough to see in the local cinema on Saturday afternoons, I replayed my way. I took the leading role, not just the female but the male as well. And if I didn't like the storyline, I just changed it around to suit. In my world I relived the events that wounded and this time I was the victor and all my enemies were publicly denounced and defeated. All in all, a most satisfactory state of affairs. I never minded going to bed early, especially on winter nights. To burrow down under the old eiderdown with the red-and-black-flowered cover and close my eyes and soar away to my own country was my delight and sleep was something that came to interrupt my dreams not to begin them.

Chapter 3: Neighbours and Friends

I am writing about a time not a place. I often walk through the Faythe today. The same houses, more or less, the same street, and yet transformed. It is just a curiosity now to say to someone from out of town, or to my sons, or their friends, "This is where I lived when I was young, this is where my brother was born, there's the house, or is it?" When I sit down like this and remove the block I suppose most people erect for protection and let the past into my conscious mind, the colours change, like a film changing from black-and-white to technicolour. I wonder why this is so? My theory is that when we are young we have an instinctive belief in good. People call it innocence, I think myself it is a gift of wisdom. So our vision is cloudless, we see not black-and-white but with a brilliance that cuts right through to the life of things, to the way things should be even if they are not. Maybe we are all born as God wants us to be. The fall is our own doing, built-in I suppose. As surely as we grow and begin to know, we warp everything, because we are too small to believe.

Goodness is too big a concept for us to grasp and so we stop believing. A child has no such problem.

When I stepped on to the street outside our house nearly fifty years ago, the warmth of our fireside did not stop with the closing of the front door. Our neighbours were a mixed bag just like all other streets in all other towns. We had the grumpy ones who seemed to hate children. The fussy old maids. The families we were warned against. The drunks, rowdies, we must have had the perverts, but such things were unknown and unnamed in my world. Right across the road from us was a public house. I know now with hindsight that the Saturday night overflow on to the streets of drunken men, only men in those days, was a ferocious indictment of the society we lived in, but to us children it was as normal as Sunday morning mass and might even afford a bit of excitement if the drunks were too rowdy and the local garda was called. We could peep out of our bedroom windows opposite and have a grandstand view of the goings-on. My mother, who certainly had no great love for drink or drunkenness in any form, having done her penance growing up in Enniscorthy with a father whose drunken escapades were legend, was very vehement in her condemnation of the said garda on one occasion. He was applying his "size twelves" with great gusto to the head of a recumbent tinker. This was pre-itinerant days and Wexford's quota of tinkers was never referred to as anything but that, with no malice or meanness intended. In those days a spade was a spade and a tinker a tinker.

Again with hindsight, I think my mother was before her time or maybe one of those women who lived outside time.

She never accepted the rigid social code of her day and we were reared with a certain freedom in that respect. Respectability, the god who ruled poorer people with a rod of iron, never reigned in our house. Indeed I think most people were held at arm's length, rich and poor alike. She seemed to have a profound suspicion of people and stood aloof. We children felt instinctively that we were somehow different from other people. I don't know why she felt that way. Probably because of her own harsh childhood and the fact that she was an "Enniscorthy Scalder" among all the "Yellow Bellies." Coupled with this inability to reach out to neighbours or friends she had a mighty heart for compassion which broke its banks at times and flowed out over friend, neighbour and enemy alike. We children lived fully, taking more than the lion's share of pleasure in the people and places around us and still hugging the difference to ourselves, like some secret bonus always there to be collected.

I was a roamer and a talker. To my mother's dismay nothing was sacred, nothing hidden. If I knew, then all knew. How often she sent me out with a warning not to divulge some bit of unimportant goings-on in our home to the neighbours only to be betrayed the minute I was in the company of a captive audience. But no great harm was ever done. We were a family with few skeletons in the closet and those that did exist were usually bones that rattled in every other closet in the street.

My cousins lived at the other end of Swan View. My mother's sister and her two daughters. As I had no sisters of my own these two girls were my constant companions. There was just enough space between us to allow us to be closer even than sisters. After all, we did not have to share either parents or possessions. To use an expression of the time, "They were better off than we were." So, I am afraid the green-eyed monster often reared its ugly head. I often raised ructions because I could not get a doll or a pram to push, or a bike, a coat, or fur gloves like my cousins. Luckily for my long-suffering mother I had a fairy godmother in the form of an aunt who lived and worked in Dublin and spent every penny of her hard-earned cash on me and my two brothers, making sure to keep us in the style to which we rapidly became accustomed.

It was in the spacious yard of these two cousins' house that my first remembered game was played. But it was more than a game to us, more a way of life. We called it "babby house" and it took up every waking minute we spent outside our own homes. We staked out a little plot, usually in an outhouse or shed, and meticulously removed the dirt and cobwebs, shining and cleaning, sweeping and arranging our "furniture" which consisted of boxes, upturned flower pots, or anything else we could move from its natural habitat. When the larger pieces were in place the real work began. We set about decorating our respective houses. Now the hunt was really on and nothing that shone or sparkled was sacred from the thieving magpies that we became. I am not speaking of valuables in any normal sense of the word. Our treasures were what we collectively referred to as "chanies". Chanies were pieces of broken crockery or glass that we foraged and dug for in every garden or dump we could reach. The joy of finding a big bit of chaney is something only a child of my time will remember. This was a time before mass production put a cheapness on everything that was more than just monetary. A piece of a broken cup or plate with a sprig of flowers adorning it or even a dot of colour or a stripe was a rare find. A piece of coloured glass was a jewel beyond price. These treasures were lovingly washed and polished and arranged in designs in the floor or walls, or back into the garden, to form our boundaries and create our own magical kingdoms where we laboured for long timeless days of pure joy. Now and then we were allowed to take real food outside. A cup of milk or a slice of bread was transformed once it entered our chaney world and became whatever we wanted it to be.

Our babby houses were moveable feasts and when one palled after days, weeks or hours depending on our humours, or how the game was progressing, we upped stakes, prised our chanies out of their resting places, took the most attractive pieces of furniture and set off for fresh fields and pastures new. Usually a different corner of the shed or yard, a couple of steps from our previous dwelling, appealed.

But I digress. I was thinking of neighbours and friends. Apart from my cousins' house there was one other house where I found a second home and that was the house of a neighbour a few doors away from our own. Here I suppose I found my first soul mate at the tender age of three. She was a gentle lady who must have been in her late thirties or forties at the time, although to me she was just Maggie. The daughter of aged parents, she was, I am now sure, that rare human being, a truly good person. Her life was simple, She kept house for her mother and father and suffered from some sort of arthritis which made her movements slow and painful. Every time I could escape from home I made for her with the sureness of a homing pigeon and she never failed me. Her smile was always there before me and her open welcome no matter what time of day I arrived. The time I spent with her in a world of snow-white table cloths spread for tea, and the ritual laying of the table in the old fashioned dining-room, was special and I knew it. I loved to help carry the food from the kitchen. How important I felt as I was given a seat at the table. There was never a mention of spillage or anything as embarrassing as bad manners. One's manners instinctively became the best in such circumstances.

Then there was the washing of the ornaments in the parlour. Every week a basin of soapy water was carefully carried into this august room and the beautiful ornaments were immersed, washed and carefully dried and replaced on highly polished surfaces. This was the time Maggie and I did all our best confiding and I could talk to my heart's content. What a listening heart she had. How much love and understanding and how instinctively I knew that no indiscreet word would ever leave this house, so there would never be hell to pay when I returned to the bosom of my own family. My mother never worried about me when I was with Maggie. She usually had to come to extricate me when she felt that even Maggie's patience and tolerance must have an end. Even today when I smell roses or see London Pride I am again in her walled garden as she gathers the best of her blooms to fill a basket for me to take to the Blessed Sacrament procession. There I took pride of place with the "strewers", the young girls who threw rose petals in front of the priest carrying the monstrance on Corpus Christi. Maggie's baskets were always the finest. How could they be anything else when they were prepared by such a one? Of course, everyone in the street was not of the same calibre as Maggie. There was the woman who copied all my mother's Fair Isle patterns. My mother had, as they say, hands to do anything. She often remarked, looking at me in a most derogatory fashion, that she did not know who she would leave her hands to. I puzzled over this remark and wondered how one left one's hands after one. Just one more mystery in the complex round of mysteries of the faith of our fathers, I supposed. Her Fair Isle knitting was much admired and envied by all and sundry and had the added bonus of being produced without the help of a pattern; she made it up as she went along. She could produce the most intricate stitches, not to mention Fair Isle versions of Donald Duck and Mickey Mouse or Roy Rogers and Trigger at the drop of a hat. We sallied forth at every festival and birthday displaying the latest creation, only to be waylaid by a neighbour with evil intent. How often I was lured into the hallway of her house by one ruse or another only to realise as the door closed behind me that I was trapped again. Then the dreaded ordeal would begin. As I hopped from one foot to another the stitches were counted and the jumper examined minutely while frantic notes and numbers were jotted down on scraps of paper. Sure enough in a matter of weeks the forgery would hit the streets and my mother would hit the roof. I was always left feeling guilty, even though I could never understand what all the fuss was about. The copy never approached the original in greatness. The colours were always wrong and the wobbly outlines never were distinguishable. One could only guess their identity while in my mother's productions every character stood out clearly and could be named at a glance.

Then there was the man whose life's work seemed to be to provoke rows with all and sundry. He was never seen to smile except when the mischief he was fanning burst into flames and there was trouble in the street. We children avoided him like the plague and took it out on his defenceless front door when we were one hundred per cent sure he was not at home. Then we would approach bravely and give a loud rat-tat-tat. On days when we were feeling extra brave, or extra vindictive, we would go so far as to kick the said doorway or even scrawl a line or two in chalk. I remember the day we misjudged so badly that as we were about our nefarious business the door was jerked open and the ogre appeared in the flesh. Such a scattering. I think I can safely say I have never moved as fast since and I was not the first one to reach the safety of the malt-house steps. These steps were our property during the day.

Here we held council meetings or just sat dejectedly waiting for the sap to rise when all our plans went astray. During the night they were inhabited by the street drunk. He would weave his way across from the pub at closing time either singing or swearing depending on his degree of fullness. He never did anything more dangerous than a spot of shadow boxing at some imaginary opponent in the middle of the street, or caused the local dogs to begin to howl with a particularly piercing rendition of *Annie Laurie* or the *Old Bog Road*. Then he would throw himself down on the malt-house steps and sleep it off until morning. He was one of the more colourful inhabitants and this was his role in life. This was what he was and we saw nothing strange about it. I suppose we drew as much comfort from hearing him make his noisy way every night as we did from the tolling of the church bells or the sound of our parents winding the clock or putting out the cat. These were the familiar, the comforting sounds of night-time in our street.

There were the very holy sisters, members of the Children of Mary, whose only contact with us was a discreet smile as they passed up and down to the sodalities, confraternities and devotions in Bride Street church. They held us in awe and we afforded them just a degree less respect than the local priests and nuns. The priests had to be saluted by the boys who went through the strange ritual of lifting their fringes when passing. Every boy in those days had a fringe, probably due to the fact that most haircuts were home-made and included the use of a pudding bowl. We girls just lowered our eyes and stepped off the path when passing the priest. In the case of the nuns, usually the sisters of St John of God hurrying to and fro in pairs to the convent school at the top of the Faythe, we were brave enough to venture a smile and maybe even a word of greeting if they happened to be two of our favourites. We had, what is only discussed today at seminars, a loving community. Why was it so easy then and so difficult now? If I was to hazard a guess I would say that life was simpler then, less complicated. We needed one another and we knew it. There was no point in pretending otherwise.

Chapter 4: The Town

Our house was one of a row of houses, some tall, some squat, some small, some smaller but all joined together with no way through to the back except through the houses themselves. Between front and back the division was more than just a length of hallway, it was all the difference in the world. The back gardens with the fields and the Rocks beyond was one world, the front, which meant the street and the town was another. The town itself was a typical small coastal town of the time, with the quay and the Main Street taking pride of place. A typical promenade in Wexford was, down the town and back up the quay, or vice-versa.

The town was still of manageable proportions in the Forties and Fifties. Each street, indeed nearly every person, known to everyone else, at least by sight and history. The boundaries were clear and most of the streets petered off into roads that quickly led to countryside. In those days the town could still plainly be seen for what it was, an encroachment on the countryside and not the opposite, as now appears to be the case with most towns and cities in our poor ravaged country. You could walk down the Folly Hill and turn up the Rocks Road and in two steps the town was behind you and the luscious countryside enfolded you. This was where we went for our picnics on days, between winter and summer, that were just warm and bright enough to stir the blood and make you want to pretend that summer was here. My mother would make sandwiches, usually banana, when this luxurious novelty could be obtained again after the war. We would take a bottle to fill with spring water at the Folly well and off with us.

The long trudge to the top of the Rocks Road was tackled slowly and peacefully. This was the time before hurry was invented. Every ditch had to be investigated and every stone turned over. Every sighting of frog spawn had to be prodded and inspected and every gate climbed. When we got to the end of the road, at the gate to yet another field, we took our seats on a particular rock that seemed to be sheltered and warmed by the sun, even on the coldest days. We set out our feast. My mother's feast was different entirely. she spent her time gazing down over the breathtaking panorama that unfolded back down below us. As the Rocks Road meandered up slowly but surely and the climb became steeper and steeper towards the end, the reward was a view of the town, the harbour and the coastline, stretching away as far as the eye could see. While my mother soaked this in we set about disturbing the peace in whatever way we chose to. A game of Cowboys and Indians was popular, for hadn't we got the real setting here, with even the authentic protests from the cows in the adjoining fields? When my mother folded her knitting and packed the straw bag we knew it was time to go. The return journey was a pure pleasure as it was all downhill and we seemed to be able to more or less roll home at a nice leisurely pace. When the Folly came into view we had just enough energy to round the corner and put on a last spurt to make it up the Faythe to our own hall-door.

These excursions were rare and bore no resemblance to the weekly route march when we went in the other direction, up the Faythe and out the Drinagh Road dressed in our best bib and tucker, protesting all the way, for the Sunday afternoon walk. How I hated this procession when most of the town seemed to be on the move in one direction or the other. Mothers and fathers and sullen-faced children, all resenting Sundays. No wonder there was such a fall away from the church. It probably had more to do with the starchy Sundays of our childhood than with any theological issues. I know Sundays in our house convinced me that God was a po-faced spoilsport. During the week we could enjoy ourselves, but on Sundays it was good clothes and woe betide you if you got a tear or a stain on anything. There was no way you could escape to the street or the garden. Everyone had to stay indoors and the only outing was the aforementioned dreaded walk, *en famille*. The one bright spot was that my long-suffering father could be depended upon to part with the coppers for sweets in Allie White's, the only shop on the Main Street open for business on Sundays by general consent.

I think the clergy had enough sense to know the cement binding the family together might not be strong enough to withstand the explosion if children were deprived of the one thing that made Sundays bearable; the paper cones of satin cushions or cloves, or aniseed balls from Allie's little shop. Mind you, there were a few renegade shopkeepers whose portals were open for an hour or two and we knew every one of them and usually managed to steer the walks in a suitable direction.

So this was Sunday. The morning time was given over to Mass-going, then there was the Sunday dinner, just as much part of the proceedings. As a matter of fact I think most women felt they were under pain of mortal sin to produce the roast beef and potatoes, the apple tart or jelly and custard, or whatever else was on the menu for the most important meal of the week. The male members of the family were champing at the bit, torn between food and football and hurling, because the second religion of Ireland took over on most Sunday afternoons; the match in the local GAA park. There was invariably a row in our house which ended with the outside slice off the still underdone roast and the smallest few roast potatoes being served up to my father as he sat on the edge of the chair at the table in the kitchen poised for flight in case he missed the opening whistle. The rest of the day was soured while my mother lamented the demise of the dinner. I never ceased to wonder why it could not all be moved up a half-hour or so but it seems that half-past one was dinner time on Sundays in Ireland and if the GAA hadn't enough sense to know this, it was not the women's fault. I wonder was it their way of opposing the only thing, apart from drink, that had as strong a hold on the men as they had?

The coal boats at the quay, the turf dump at the other side of town, Pierce's Foundry, the Timber Company, these were the sources of work for most men in our street. Fathers disappeared early in the morning and came home in the late evening. Pierce's Horn, which sounded at half past five in the evening, was the signal for us that play-time was nearly over and we would soon be called for our tea.

The shops were small, and usually family-owned concerns, before the advent of the supermarket. Indeed when I was a child a supermarket would have been as foreign a concept as space travel or motor cars outside everyone's door. The pace of life was slow and natural and the modern disease of stress was unheard of.

Wexford lost a big percentage of its men and young people to England, indeed England seemed closer to us than Dublin. We were more used to waving goodbye at the Pier Head as the boat left for England or meeting people at the south station on their return.

It seems to me that the town fell in with our plans when we were children. It opened up to us little by little as we needed it, providing new places as we moved further from home, giving countryside and seaside when the season was right and closing in protectively around us when we grew tired and needed to retreat to our own place at the end of the year.

Chapter 5: The Street

This morning I am thinking back to when I was a child in the Faythe and what the street meant to me. Again, I am made aware that a child's view is clear and clean and its attitude brings all the harmony and peace necessary for joyous living.

Each day is a complete life in itself and all the worn out clichés of adult life are facts in the child's mind. There is no worry about tomorrow because it is too far off to be thought about and yesterday is forgotten in the excitement of a new day. There is, as yet, no ability to feel guilt or any great anxiety. Fears, if they exist at all, are only of bogey men or banshees, the real fears of adult life have not as yet intruded – after all, why should a child be afraid of life itself, for isn't it still the great untasted adventure stretching out ahead in an endless glorious wending way? I don't think I am glorifying the past when I say that as children in the street we lived out effortlessly everything the adult world now strives in vain to achieve. We were one, we were classless, we devoted our time with a single-mindedness that was total to enjoying and savouring every minute of the daylight and freedom we were allowed. And our wars were only pretend, with no injuries inflicted and all prisoners returned unharmed when dusk came, and mothers with it, to claim their own.

we were vaguely aware that some of us were stronger than others. One boy in particular had weak eyes and was thin and angular and could not run as fast as the rest of us, but he had something else that compensated and put him maybe a bit ahead of the rest; a silver gun in a white holster he wore strapped to his hip at all times, and steel tips on his shoes that produced sparks when he struck his feet against the side of the path. He was a quiet boy and easily accepted by all – maybe he was put upon a little – he was always the first hostage taken to be tied to the lamppost and the last to be released but he never seemed to mind and if he did he never complained loudly enough to make any difference. He had the distinction of having an aunt who actually returned from America, not once, but many times, a rarity in those days when a voyage to America was usually a one-way affair. This aunt came bearing gifts, and apart from his much-envied silver gun, he was the proud possessor of a number of hats and caps – I definitely remember an African sun-helmet and a peaked naval captain's cap among others.

As I was an only girl with an elder and a younger brother, I took my place with the boys – a place that had to be fought for and bargained for not once, but many times and one that involved a lot of compromise.

My older brother had two particular friends and I usually tagged along and was more or less accepted, though times it was an uneasy truce that existed between us. We all moved together in a loose band and the boundaries of the street were clearly defined. Castle Hill Street at the top corner where the street led down to Barrack Street and on to South Main Street – the Folly Hill at the bottom corner and Lar Doyle's shop at the top of our row of houses. Beyond these points we never moved until the older lads came of age and then by some unspoken permission we wandered further afield – down to Parnell Street and up to the top of the Faythe and the Rocks Lane. But our own patch seemed to hold all we needed and by mutual consent we stayed there, changing our game with the seasons or the humours we were in and playing from morning until night, only taking time off to reluctantly return home for refuelling when it became absolutely necessary.

The first games I remember were the ones that involved catching and being caught. "Tig," we called it, and it involved dividing into two gangs and each gang choosing a lamppost. At a given signal we all ran – I don't remember how we defined the pursued and the pursuers, but if you were caught you were lashed to the opposing gang's lamppost and the game ended when one gang was caught and successfully tied up.

Who knows how the birds know when it is suddenly time to build nests or to start practising for the long flight to foreign shores? The same instinct may have been responsible for the sudden appearance on our streets of spinning tops and whips, or sticks and wheels, or taws or any number of items that appeared at regular intervals. I only know that some morning, or maybe evening, a lone child would appear with a wooden spinning top and a piece of twine tied to a short stick and proceed to spin his top and whip it up and down the street and within hours, or next morning, the street, as if by magic, would be filled with industry and every child set to whipping with a will. Last year's tops were produced and if they could not be found, the shops, by the same magic, were suddenly full of wooden tops of all shapes and sizes. This craze lasted for a certain period of time and then the whips were removed from the ends of the sticks and the sticks themselves used to bowl wheels of all descriptions up and down where the tops had lately been.

An excursion to the Rocks the local quarry, saw us returning with pockets full of chalk – or rocks that made marks on the paths and roads, and then the heck-a-beds started. This could only be played outside "safe-houses," that is, houses whose occupants were kindly disposed to children and could overlook the chalk-beds and hieroglyphics marked on the paths outside their houses and the noise of children endlessly hecking on one foot, propelling at the same time a large flat stone or an empty polish tin when it could be procured. These hecking games were none too popular with parents because of what they usually did to the toes of even the sturdiest shoes in little or no time. The heck-a-beds were the first real taste of sexual discrimination to be introduced into our lives, because even though the girls were allowed to play Cowboys and Indians, Tig, and all the other games (though it must be stated there were usually more than a fair share of female Indians), the boys drew the line at heck-a-beds and it was nearly always an all-female occupation and if some of the quieter lads joined in it drew down the dreaded cry of "sissy" on their heads. When you saw crowds of men gathered in the lane at the top of the street or in Pat Molloy's field you knew there was a game of Pitch and Toss in progress – when you saw the children gathered in this lane or on any patch of bare earth you knew it was taw-time. We played "taws" or "marbles" with the same ferocity we applied to every other activity. The coloured taws were treasured and the steelers (probably ball-bearings) were an especial prize. A circle was drawn in the earth and taws placed at intervals around it – a line was drawn where we knelt and flicked our biggest and best "red-nellies" trying to remove the taws from the circle. There were various shots; one with the peculiar name of "cackie-knuckle" comes to mind, and we became deadly in aim and accuracy. So for a long time each child travelled the length and breath of the street with a little cloth purse full of marbles or a pocket full of the same, seeking out the best games with as much eagerness as Damon Runyon's characters looking for a crap game at around the same era in far-off New York.

An event that changed our lives and certainly our games was when a relation of ours got a job in the Capital Cinema. I don't know what her status was, but she carried a large silver torch and lit the way for late comers to their seats and also allowed my brother and myself to sit in the expensive seats while only paying the two pence entry fee to the "gods" or the pit as it was called. Maybe this distinction sewed the first seeds of snobbery in my young soul, because one felt in some way exalted entering the hallowed ground at the top of the cinema and the hordes of young people in the lower extremities of the house became inferior. I know on the rare occasions when we frequented the second picture house in the town – the Cinema Palace in Cinema Lane – commonly known as the "Hop and Scratch" (for obvious reasons!) and were consigned to the nether regions for our tuppence, I invariably felt an acute sense of shame and tried to think myself invisible when the lights came up. Anyhow, this bargain ticket presented quite a problem for my mother who was none too keen on the Saturday matinees, yet never a woman to bypass a bargain. Her thrifty side won out and my brother and myself joined the queue of excited children every Saturday afternoon at two o'clock. Thus began a passionate love affair with celluloid that took over our very souls and possesses us both to this day. No matter what golden oldie is shown on TV, I have seen it before – so much so that my husband has often wondered if I spent my entire youth in the local cinema, and my brother is a respected "Film Buff" whose knowledge of the golden days of the silver screen is boundless.

For me the darkened picture house opened up a new and glorious avenue of escape into other worlds. Buck Jones, Hopalong Cassidy and Gabby Hayes, Roy Rogers and the rest, made us so familiar with the Wild west that we could go home at five o'clock, gather the rest of the gang around us and recreate the matinee in Pat Molloy's field in living colour and stereophonic sound before the Hollywood moguls ever thought of it. I never had the problem of being "the girl", because with unspoken agreement all romantic bits were consigned to the cutting-room floor and I could safely gallop over the hillocks, beating my behind with my hand to spur on my trusty horse and shouting, "Bang bang!" (well actually, we made a much more realistic sound but I cannot reproduce it here). My brother always assured me that even though I had to pretend to be the "baddie" most of the time, it was really one of the other fellows, usually our friend of the silver gun and holster, who was in fact the villain. He could not be told in case he refused to join in and this would create difficulties because the silver gun and holster were now strapped around my brother's waist. What a negotiator he was – I often wonder why he never became a politician! So depending on the film we viewed, our games could be situated in any part of the world and we became familiar with the Hollywood version of the east, the west and the Bible among other things. In summer we spent days digging a hole in our garden – the top part that was never used to grow anything. This was no ordinary hole, but a carefully designed excavation that became a boat with seats where we re-fought the naval battles of World War II and even some of World War I.

When we tired of this we moved up to the rocks and made camps with dried bracken. Wonderful forests and desert islands and all sorts of exotic sets took shape in the woods and rocks beyond Pat Molloy's field. Thank God I have never actually revisited these places as an adult and most of them are long gone now from the actual world, but they still exist intact in my memory – not ghostly and shabby like the back lots in Metro-Goldwyn-Mayer, but still in glorious technicolour and vibrant with sound and life.

Chapter 6: Lights of Other Days

To counteract the images on the screen, a liberal supply of flesh and blood characters peopled our town and indeed our street. These men and women were part of our lives and an important part, because they were the very real people that life throws up. The marginal people, pared down by living, so that they stood out in clear relief with all the phoniness removed.

As children we accepted them quite naturally, they neither frightened nor repelled us and maybe because we lived in a gentler. quieter time, we picked up very few fears from our elders. This was a time when people believed misfortune of any kind was a touch of the hand of God and paid a strange respect to those afflicted by it in any way.

I remember looking out my bedroom window in the morning and seeing a black bundle of humanity sitting on the steps of the old graveyard at the top of Castle Hill Street – this was "Black Lead", a man of such benign countenance that even though he was threatened on us all by harassed mothers, we had no fear, and the cry of: "Black Lead will get you," left us all unmoved. I suppose he was Wexford's answer to Dublin's "Johnny Forty- Coats." He wore so many tattered coats he really was as broad as he was long. A small rotund figure, his top coat, a long gabardine of ancient vintage, and his blackened face topped by a black hat of uncertain pedigree – it could have been a top-hat in some previous life or a fedora – I never got close enough to find out.

This apparition appeared at fairly regular intervals and took up his position on the graveyard steps where he remained night and day until one morning, when he vanished as silently as he had appeared. I often watched him produce some pieces of food from his ragged pockets and eat a solitary picnic, smiling away to himself as he chewed. We never had any conversation with him – just silently observed from a respectable distance, or played around him while he observed us.

Rumour had it that he was a famous artist who had chosen the nomadic life and the black hands and face were the result of the paints he used for his work. A more mundane reason for his dusky hands and face was said to be that he rubbed black lead into his skin to preserve it and keep out the cold.

Then there was the slightly more sinister figure called "Brass Bullet" who flitted around the perimeters of our lives and was instinctively avoided. We were never warned off in words, but we probably picked up the vibes and made ourselves scarce when he appeared.

A quaint couple straight out of the pages of Dickens was "Paddy Go Back" and his spouse. Paddy was a tiny little man who wore a tweed suit with a cloth cap and sported a small moustache. His wife was a gaunt crone with a long yellow face – dressed in a black Twenties-style coat trailing down to her ankles and topped off with a mud-coloured, pull-on cloche hat. She had the look of a large black crow or one of Walt Disney's famous buzzards. This strange pair were often to be seen promenading down the Faythe, but never side by side. Paddy always walked two or three steps behind his bride in true Prince Philip style and if he tried to overtake, she would be heard to growl, "Go back Paddy – go back", hence the nickname. There were two versions of the story – one was that Paddy had been untrue and his punishment had to be seen by all, forever-more, he was to follow at a respectable distance.

Another version was that they were misers and scanned the path for any valuables – a piece of coal, a coin – then if she passed it, Paddy would be sure to spot it and could call out, "Drop on it, Maggie" – which she promptly did. Whichever yarn was true we called out both directives every time the hapless couple hove into sight and then we ran for cover though what retribution we feared from poor old "Paddy Go Back" and the missus I don't know. Maybe the prospect of being chased by the two old crones was enough.

One of the most lovable characters of all was a lad we all knew as "Jemmie". Jemmie was what was referred to then as a little soft in the head but he was the happiest inhabitant of our town – he had a long loping walk, somewhat reminiscent of Groucho Marx, but in his actions, dress and general behaviour he was more like the other brother – Harpo. Jemmie spent most of his time roaming the streets and joining in, usually in dumb show, with any activity that took his fancy, but the real love of his life was a parade and a band.

On St Patrick's Day, or any time when people marched, Jemmie was out front leading the crowd and he was accepted by all and sundry as part of the proceedings. I don't think any parade would have been complete without this ragged, comical figure. Local dignitaries took no notice of him as he proceeded along, waving and smiling to the onlookers. One of my longest and most endearing memories of his antics happened when an effort was made to upgrade our St Patrick's Day Parade. One of the nearby towns had a pipe band, all swirling pipes and twirling kilts and in those pre- Americanised days when dancing bands and majorettes were a thing of the future this band was famous all over the country. By some method, probably monetary, they were enticed from their own town and hired to lead the Wexford Parade and the whole town was agog with excitement. Somebody must have decided that in honour of the occasion Jemmie had to be dispensed with and when he came along to sidle into his usual position he was warned off in no uncertain manner. The parade gathered at the far side of the Faythe – the usual route was up the Faythe at one side, a smart turn and back down the other side and down the Main Street – so we had a vantage point from our own front door.

The band was certainly impressive – fine tall men with kilts and busbies and the finest of all was the leader who took his place well out in front, staff in hand ready to lead off the whole affair. After the usual huffing and puffing the swirl of pipes arose and they were off up along the Faythe. Such a sight and sound had never been seen or heard and there had not been so much excitement since Big Jim Larkin spoke from the back of a cart on that very spot in 1911, the time of the lockout in Pierce's Foundry. As the band wheeled sharply to come back down the street the leader twirled the long slender staff in his hands getting ready to toss it in the air. This was his *piece de resistance* and something we were all waiting with bated breath to see. Every eye was trained on him and he knew it – this was his moment in the sun – but just at the crucial moment there was a scuffle at the side of the path, just up from our door, and a ragged figure broke from the crowd. With raincoat flapping, head down and knees bent, Jemmie ran out to take his rightful position, and this time he meant business. With a long stick in his hand he turned and grinned at the usurper and with a flourish tossed the stick in the air and caught it as it descended, which was more than our busbied friend did, Jemmie's timing was impeccable – he had broken from the ranks just as the staff had left the large man's hands to spin into the air, and so, his attention diverted for a moment at the interruption, he missed his catch and with a clatter it hit the ground in front of him. There was a gasp from the crowd, the swirling pipes faltered slightly and the great man had to bend to retrieve his fallen staff. But Jemmie never faltered – he proceeded with head held high waving his stick and acknowledging the cheers of the children who were only vaguely aware of the awfulness of the event and the dinge in the dignity of the visiting stars, not to mention the town fathers. All we knew was that Jemmie had scored a bull's-eye and his joy was infectious. Officialdom bowed to the inevitable and Jemmie set off as usual – hitting new heights in his leaping and capering as the bagpipes roared out behind him.

"Maggie Mallen sells fish,

Three ha'pence a dish

Cut their heads off, cut their tails off

Maggie Mallen sells fish"

This was repeated in our street more often than Baa Baa Black Sheep, but then every child knew Maggie Mallen. A little dumpy figure who had indeed got a feather in her hat , long black skirts and a shawl around her shoulders as she walked along behind her cart selling fresh fish straight from the boats at the quay. Many's the time I stood at the back of the cart while she slapped the little flat fishes onto the plate in my hands. Then, after handing her the couple of pence payment, I would carry them carefully back across the street to where my mother would gut them and cook them for our dinner.

When Maggie Mallen called out, "Fresh fish!" she was telling the truth.

We never had to be encouraged to recycle our bottles. Indeed houses and gardens were scoured for bottles or jars and when Ben Fenlon's cry, "Rags, bones and bottles!" rent the air we would descend on him with our cache of glass. It was one of our main sources of income as we were rewarded with a halfpenny for four jars or four bottles, and a halfpenny was a halfpenny then. Ben lived in a house in the Rocks Lane and we often spent long hours hidden behind the wall opposite his house observing his activities. He was a fine tall man who bore, as my mother used to say, "the relics of auld dacency". He had obviously seen better days but now his only companion seemed to be the old horse who pulled his cart load of "rags and bones". We often watched him securing his front door which was padlocked with not one but many locks of all descriptions. He would carefully use all the keys on his huge key-ring to secure doors and windows and then walk around to the side and throw the bunch of keys back into his bed through the space where the end wall of his house should have been! Apart from our very own characters we had the annual visitors – the travellers, the colourful people, the last of the dispossessed I suppose. One man arrived annually, unrolled a little mat at the top of the street and then proceeded to twist himself into a human knot. He remained in this position for a certain length of time, then unravelled himself and moved his mat down to the middle of the street and proceeded to knot his knees round his neck again. This performance was gazed on with awe by all of us and he usually managed to collect a few coppers – it must have been worth his while because he turned up at regular intervals.

The Indian who sold pins and bric-a-brac from a large suitcase, the gypsy woman who sold lace from a large basket and read palms if you were so inclined, these were all part of the yearly cycle. Then as time moved on and things became more sophisticated we began to get more organised visitors. I remember "Ima Weight", the fat lady who took a room in the Quay and we children were allowed in for a penny to view her folds of fat as she sat on a mat glowering into space. Rumour had it that she was exposed as a fraud in England when a man stuck a pin into one of her many spare tyres.

"Tom Thumb" came, not the original I am sure, but a little gent who was trying to turn his lack of inches to advantage. He left us singularly unimpressed.

The Indian Rope Trick was a favourite and there was a floodlit exhibition in Pat Molloy's field by a man who leaped from a small platform up on a pole and landed in a small bath of water. My father was very impressed by this performance and came home in a state of high excitement shortly afterwards to report that the same trick had backfired in Carlow and the man had broken his neck. We were not surprised.

Well, the light of heaven to him and to all that motley collection who helped to make our town what it was, in those bygone days, when I was young.

Chapter 7: Spring

When I was a child I could smell the approach of spring, but then so could most of the children in our street. While adults were still huddled at the fire, swaddled in heavy winter clothing, and gales still lashed the houses with winter fervour; we would raise our heads and sniff, like dogs smelling the wind, and suddenly announce we were getting into our ankle-socks next day. The ensuing battle between mothers wielding woollen socks and winter coats resounded from most houses from around the beginning of March, but by St Patrick's Day we had usually won the war and our milk-bottle legs appeared under sensible coats. Even though the white ankle-socks looked rather incongruous with heavy leather shoes, we were happy – the flags were up, spring was officially here.

I often wonder did we draw it out of winter's womb before its time with our longing or did an obliging God know we had exhausted winter's treasures and taken pity on our eagerness? Doors opened and children spilled out to inspect the ravages of the previous few months and to re-establish their rights on the street and in the fields behind the houses. What a world we found waiting. Who can forget the first foray into a still winter-gripped field, the first tentative exploration of the trees and hedges and, most of all, the first finds. A few primroses under a bush caught at the heart and stopped us in our tracks, a clump of early cowslips made us sing, the sight of a bird entering a hedge trying to look inconspicuous was enough to tip us the wink that there was a nest close at hand. The distinctive smell of the yellow furze in my own lane now has the power to transport me back to where I wandered the fiends and rocks with the first friend I made outside the street. Her people had a farm in a spot just outside the town. Its land had all the rocks and crannies and little untidy hedged-in fields that farms had before people became so greedy for land and reduced the whole countryside to vast dull square meadows with barbed wire fences instead of hedges and little rock walls.

My brother who had a bicycle before most of the rest of us in the street would give me a lift to my friend's house whenever I was allowed and he would deposit me thankfully and make his escape – sure of a few hours respite from my interference. My friend Peggy and I roamed the fields, picking flowers to our hearts' content, huge bunches of bluebells, cowslips, primroses.

Who would have believed then that we were on the threshold of an age when even the wild flowers would be in danger of disappearing from the face of the earth? There was one spot in particular, we reached by following a narrow path through briars and furze to the top of a little rocky hill, where we set up camp and organised a tentative "Babby House" in the open air. How many hours we spent there I could not even guess at, but without realising it, I soaked in a love of the countryside that was to draw me back in later years from the heart of the city to set up my own tentative "Babby House" in a near derelict country cottage – but that's another story. Here too I got my love for dogs. There were always dogs on the farm and how can you ever have a fear of them in adult life when you have dressed a spaniel pup in a doll's dress and pushed him around a field in a doll's pram? My father was a great man to find a bird's nest and my first glimpse into one was when he lifted me up on his shoulder and gently parted the leaves to point out the little speckled eggs with a dire warning never to touch them. He told me if I were so bold as to even put my fingers on to them the mother bird would get my scent and abandon the nest without hatching out her chicks. I don't know if this was true or not but it had the desired effect. The older people instilled a love of nature and a respect for it into us by their example without our being aware of it happening and most children at that time had an instinctive attitude of preservation and care. There were a few exceptions of course and one of the saddest things in the world was to find a "chucked nest" with the eggs robbed or crushed on the ground, or the newly emerged chicks dead with their necks broken.

We carried home frog-spawn, thus ensuring a plentiful supply of frogs in our garden at a later date.

We had an old tin bath in the yard and filled with water and with a bit of wood balanced on the side; this made an ideal swimming pool for frogs. We stalked the bigger ones and caught them. The trick is to let the frog move into your open hand, placed on the ground in front of him, and then close it gently around his neck – firmly cupping the other hand over him. Thus frog-napped, our quarry would be borne triumphantly back to the yard and shown his new temporary home. We spent long soggy days forcing our new pets to dive from higher and higher boards and race across the bath. They always obliged and I don't think much harm was done because we always set them free when the game was over and allowed them to return to the wilds of the cabbage patch. Mind you, it was whispered that two fellows from another street had done the unspeakable and blown two poor frogs up like a barrage balloon only to see them burst before their very eyes, but we all hoped it was only a rumour.

Spring was gardening time and as surely as the children erupted from the front doors the men emerged from the back and set to with a will, digging and getting ground that had been turned over and left to winter in ice and snow, ready to receive the vegetables and potatoes to see us through another year. I had an uncle, my mother's brother, a big strong, gentle country man from Enniscorthy, who came most years to take over our garden. My father was not a great man to raise a sweat at any activity, least of all gardening. It was my mother who had the green fingers. Many's the time I watched Bill sowing the potatoes – making the drills even and straight, filling them with manure and lovingly laying the seed potatoes along before covering them in and patting the sides firm with his shovel. He was a born gardener – he loved his work. He also had red hair and a temper to match. Many's the good row I witnessed between him and our cantankerous neighbour. This neighbour's garden ran parallel with ours and we shared a grassy path up along the side. Being more than a bit of a mischief-maker he never failed to try to rise Bill and usually the bait used was this famous path which he claimed we were always trying to cut away at our side to enlarge our holding. As the gardens were vast anyhow and only part of ours was even cultivated, this accusation was ridiculous, but it never failed to get Bill going. I remember one night when he told our neighbour in a long and colourful monologue what exactly he could do with his path, ending with the sentiment that it was a pity he could not roll it up at night and take it indoors with him for safe keeping.

Mixed up with the good memories of gardens and new potatoes in my mind, is a dark picture of gloom and much suffering and misery. It was that same uncle who, when reaching across for the milk at supper time after an evening's work at the spuds, knocked a mug of scalding tea over on to my arm. What I remember most vividly about the event was not the pain, but the reaction of the adults. The noise and the panic frightened me more than the actual scalding. My father got to me first and pushed up the sleeve of my red knitted jumper. Unfortunately the scalded skin peeled off my arm with it and hung like a curtain flapping. I was rushed to the nearest expert who happened to be a chemist not noted for his sobriety. We caught him on a bad night and he just cut the skin off and slapped a bandage on the scalded arm. I was to suffer long and hard for his folly. A year later found me with two bandaged arms; the first one having become ulcerated, affected the other one, and it was many a long day before my poor flesh healed and saw the light again.

Easter left very few memories with me. I don't really know why, maybe the religion of my childhood Ireland put more emphasis on crucifixion than resurrection. I do remember a great spurt of industry one Holy Week when my mother set about producing home-made Easter eggs for our delectation. I don't think they were a great success, maybe because the process involved emptying the whole eggshell by the precarious method of sticking a pin into it and inducing the contents out through the tiny hole – like siphoning petrol, one had to first suck to set the operation in motion and a mouth full of raw egg is just as noxious as a mouth full of petrol if the job goes wrong. Being a very determined woman, my mother ignored the mound of broken shells and kept going until she had the finished article. I don't know how she managed to fill the empty shell with the melted chocolate or where she got this at the time because it was during the war when such luxuries were thin on the ground, to say the least!

I remember one woman shaming the whole community by telling out on the Wilfred Pickles Show, on the illustrious occasion when the great man visited Wexford, how she had rescued a fried egg which had fallen off the pan into the turf fire, dusted it off and served it up to her unsuspecting husband. Her contemporaries, for whom this was probably only a very minor culinary sin, never forgave her for proclaiming it in public, and on the wireless too, to be broadcast across the water where we all knew we were looked on as gombeens anyhow.

The rituals of May with its devotion to the Blessed Virgin Mary was much more to our liking. There was something we could really understand, there was no mystery about the fact that a mother was a VIP in any man's language and the Mother of God had the edge on all other mothers. Every house had a May altar with candles and flowers in front of the familiar blue and white statue. My own mother was always a bit reluctant, candles and candle grease were one of her pet hates (the other two were knife drawers and button boxes – both these receptacles were anathema to her for some strange reason). But we persisted and decked our altar out with all the trimmings. It usually glowed with love and care for at least a week or two before we lost interest.

These were the glorious evenings of the May devotions when the whole population of Maudlintown and the Faythe, the females anyhow, began to drift down any time after half past six, to the Church of the Assumption in Bride Street to join in the Rosary and Benediction for the month of May. Ah! the joy of gathering all your religious paraphernalia into your best handbag and setting off for Bride Street. I often muse now on the lack of interest shown by the young in any church activity – too much competition, I suppose. But for us children it was a great source of enjoyment and we fought to be allowed to go unfettered by any adult attention. I remember the first year I was allowed to make the trip with an older girl, I must have been about six years old and my prized possession was a pink plastic shoulder bag shaped like a heart. This bag was crammed with holy pictures of all shapes and sizes collected from God knows where – probably Christmas cards or old prayer books or presented by the good nuns as a reward for bringing a penny for the black babies. Once safely ensconced in front of the altar in Bride Street the swapping began and all the saints of the Holy Roman Empire along with their Irish brethren were viewed and bargained for and their value was as keenly fixed and haggled over as the value of the punt on today's foreign market. Of course the Good Lord was number one – especially when depicted as a young baby or boy complete with golden halo and three fingers raised in blessing. The Holy Mother in all her various costumes came next and St. Patrick in full canonicals ran a close third. All swapping had to close when the priest entered the pulpit and started the Rosary, but I am afraid we were often drawn back to the first order of business in spite of the tut-tutting of the old ladies kneeling around us. Even sometimes whispered threats and dire warnings of word being carried back to our parents about our nefarious dealings in the Temple failed to stop us. How the good God must have enjoyed it all. I have absolutely no doubts that the God who created the warthog has enough fun in Him to enjoy the antics of six-year-old imitation women in short white gloves and berets, with pink plastic shoulder bags full of what passed as pictures of the Communion of Saints.

Ah! Bride Street, with its magnificent altar, lit by what seemed to a child's eyes to be thousands of candles, blazing like the courts of Heaven itself and the smell of incense wafting in the air as the priest intoned the beautiful Latin words of the Tantum Ergo. Even today when I sit there in silence – though the beautiful altar is no more, a victim to the early excesses of post-Vatican Two zeal to do away with graven-images – I close my eyes and I am six years old again. My parents, neighbours and friends are all around me – not cold ghosts, but warm vibrating presences as real as the six-year-old child in the centre of my being and I have no difficulty believing in the resurrection of the body and the Life Everlasting.

Chapter 8: Summer

The coming of summer was like keeping the good wine until last. Already sated with the joys of spring we felt that life could offer nothing more; then the first golden days of summer burst upon us, whipping us into new heights of discovery and creativity. The cold stone had left the water by the second week in June and so swimming could now be added to the long list of things to do. But it was not so easy to get to the sea in those days and the Kaats Strand and Ferrybank left a lot to be desired. Even Ardcavan was unpredictable and one often had to walk out miles to get enough water to sit in. So the street and the gardens were where we spent most of our very young summers.

I remember the tar in the Faythe melting under my toes when I discarded my sandals and ran bare-footed and free with flagrant disregard for safety and orders from barracks! Bicycles usually made their appearance and any child lucky enough to possess one could usually be depended upon to share especially when a little pressure or bribery was brought to bear. I learned to ride on a little blue bicycle belonging to some other child. Round and round the square I went while one of the older boys, a lovely quiet, patient lad, held on to the back of the saddle. How well I remember the moment when I looked back to see him far behind me and realised I was on my maiden solo voyage. A brief moment of exhilaration and then, like Peter walking on the water, I looked down and that was it. I ended up on the ground with two bloody knees and the bicycle on top of me. But I persevered and was soon tearing around the Faythe on my brother's bike. Because I was too small to get my leg over the bar I had to stoop under it and hold the bike at a very precarious angle. I could say I became not only a cyclist but a trick-cyclist in record time. "When needs must", as my mother was fond of saying "the Devil drives."

Hot weather meant sandals, no runners in those days, and sandals in our house meant Clarks, no cheap imitations. Because young feet grew quickly sandals were usually purchased at least one size too big so the first few weeks of summer found us with blistered heels and sore toes. The offending articles were usually discarded, especially when we reached the haven of the grassy fields. Now hot lazy days also called for new games to keep us occupied and happy, without having to exert too much physical energy. My brother's rich imagination and inventive streak could usually be relied on to come up with the goods. I remember one game he thought up which raced through our street like a fever and soon spread to the adjoining streets and gangs of children. Probably inspired by the Pitch and Toss the men played, this game was simplicity itself and there was no cash outlay needed. He simply got an old shoe box and cut a small hole in the top, then he gathered all the stout bottle-tops he could find. This involved a few daring daylight raids round the back of the local pubs where the treasure was to be found. As this holy ground was definitely off-limits for respectable children we took our life in our hands and usually went on horseback and with handkerchiefs over our faces.

We descended on the rubbish heaps at the back of Danny Morgan's pub like Jesse James and the boys approaching the bank in Dodge City and carried off our booty with slick professionalism and very few casualties. The idea of the game was to try to pitch the bottle-tops into the hole in the shoe box. If they went in, the owner of the box had to pay out on the double but any that fell short were collected and added to the box owner's treasure.

For a short time my brother was the sole owner but then, as is the case with all schemes, the entrepreneurial spirit began to move and more and more of us had our own boxes and small stake of tops. Soon there were, as they say, all chiefs and no Indians, so we had to go further afield. One morning we descended on Parnell Street and set up shop in the back lane. The local children were enticed to join in and soon the game had caught on and business was booming. We returned home that evening flushed with success having denuded Parnell Street and its environs of anything that even vaguely resembled bottle-tops.

We were nothing if not inventive and our games were all home-produced because in those days money was a scarce commodity. It had not achieved the central position it holds today and was available for the essentials only. Whatever about our elders, we children accepted this as a rule of life and got on with the business of living *sans capital*.

One summer when I was very young my mother decided to "Get out of chickens". This was probably due to the fact that her stock had been seriously depleted a short time before. She had a shed in the yard which housed her hens and one was the proud mother of a dozen or so chicks that had been hatched out on the premises. Today's children would probably delight over these little furry balls of yellow and brown feathers but to us it meant one thing – work. The hens had to be marched down the yard every day and through a hole in the back wall out into a run in the garden where they could be left to their own pursuits until dusk when the battalion had to be regrouped and paraded back to the hen-house again. Woe betide us if we forgot this task. Now don't believe anyone who tries to tell you hens are stupid, they are not. They are clever, mean and devious pests. Just because they stick their heads into the nearest ditch at the first sniff of trouble doesn't mean they are thick. On the contrary, they know someone has to carry the can for their safety and they just stay there, bottoms in the air, waiting to be rescued.

While the chicks were young they had to receive special attention and my brother and I had to take turns watching them while they took the air for an hour or two with the other hens. There was a hard wooden seat opposite the hen-run and here we sat while on duty, fortified with the Beano or the Dandy and a few fistfuls of gooseberries or loganberries from the bushes in the yard. One fateful day my brother was left in charge and out marched the proud mother hen with her brood in tow. Vincent was so engrossed, in the antics of Desperate Dan and the boys, that he failed to see the large black tomcat from next door lying lazily along the wall beside the hen-run trying to look nonchalant. He always swore that the cat never budged but he must have missed its lightning strikes because when his watch was over the brood was reduced to four chicks and a puzzled mother hen and there was nothing to be seen but a few desolate yellow feathers here and there, grim evidence of the fate of the rest of the little band. It took him a long time to talk himself out of that one and luckily I was away at the top of the street on some business of my own that day so I had no share of the blame.

This episode must have disheartened my mother because shortly after that the shed was cleaned out and the run dismantled. I don't know where the remaining hens went, maybe they were served up to us in disguise.

The empty hen-house was seized upon immediately by myself and my younger brother and we moved in after removing as much evidence of the previous occupants as we could. At this stage we were coming seriously under the influence of the American heroes because big consignments of American comics were arriving into the town, usually sent home by uncles and aunts or older brothers and sisters in the States. I discovered later in my life that what we treasured and bargained for and swapped our copies of comics for were part of American newspapers, the funnies. One of the characters was Captain Marvel, a super caped crusader who splattered his enemies all over the pages with captions like Krash – Klunk – Splosh etc. In one publication we got one of our most daring ideas, we would start up a Captain Marvel Club, and where better to start it than in the lately vacated hen-house.

The membership was to be seriously vetted and we made our first major mistake when we blackballed my older brother and his sidekicks as he was seriously out of grace with us for some bit of mischief against our possessions. The password was "Niatpac Levram" which to the uninitiated is the great man's name spelled backwards. The other condition of membership was to have a cape so most local women were short an apron on afternoons when our meetings were in session. The club did not live up to the great expectations we had of it. Some of the blame for its early demise was due to the harassment we got from the people who were barred and spent most of the time outside the door making chicken noises and other derogatory comments while we tried to discuss relevant business inside. But I think what really put the tin hat on it altogether was when one of our members in a burst of zeal tried to launch himself into the air off the top of his own outside lavatory with his mother's blue-and-white spotted apron billowing out behind him. Maybe if he had not shouted "Shazam!" at the exact moment his feet left *terra firma* his parents would not have made the connection. Sadly our chicken-house doors had to be closed on what had promised to be a worthy alma mater for budding adventurers.

Chapter 9: Rosslare

The road to heaven, on balmy summer days when I was young, was the steel railway track pointing out of the South Station towards Rosslare. In those days Rosslare bore little resemblance to the streamlined seaside resort that exists today, with its luxury hotels, bustling caravan parks, cafés and places of amusement.

In our day, it was a placid sandy village by the sea, lazily snoozing in the summer heat, rolling over pleasantly to accommodate the bathers, like a dog in the sunshine too happy to be bothered by fleas.

My first visit there was with my cousin and her two aunts, her father's sisters. They carried us on the back of their bicycles and when I look at faded snapshots of those days now and see two smiling young women and two fat toddlers in knitted swimsuits, one red-haired, one dark, I can still feel the heat of the lino in the little wooden hut they owned in Duggan's field and the roughness of the sand we carried in on our still wet feet after our days on the beach. The fields beside the sea were nearly deserted then – just cows too busy munching to be disturbed and here and there a few hens scratching in the sandy grass. It was so peaceful that one could hear the noise of the waves lapping the shore. This soothing background music, together with the heat of the sun induced a sort of torpor that led on to an existential state. No wonder the summer days seemed endless then and always clear and sunny. There was nothing to break the clean line, no sound, no fury, and we were suspended outside ourselves and allowed to observe. Maybe the good God wanted us to catch and hold something within us. He knew what we did not, that all this was soon to end and we would enter a time when sand and sea, peace and tranquillity would not be enough and would have to be sacrificed to the great God "Progress". All such thoughts were far from our minds when we coaxed and cajoled our mother to come to Rosslare on the train. When we succeeded and she agreed we gathered our buckets and spades, our togs and tackle and stood champing at the bit while she packed the necessary provisions and then we were away – running ahead of her down Castle Hill Street, down Parnell Street and into the station to wait for the train to arrive from the North Station on the other side of the quay.

No wonder children called it the puff-puff, because that's exactly what it was – the old steam-engine that eventually chugged its way towards us. But of course we saw it as a huge monster thundering along spewing smoke from every orifice and the only thing that induced me to enter it at all in my very young days was the prospect of a day at the sea.

The train was a familiar sight in the Wexford of the Forties and Fifties as it meandered across the wooden works from the North to South of the town and it was quite a common sight to see someone descend from the moving train and proceed across to one of the shops on the quay for a box of matches or a packet of cigarettes or some other forgotten message and then stroll back and re-enter the carriage before the train crossed Crescent Quay. I suppose the whistles it gave when going its merry way was more in greeting than to warn strollers on the wooden works of its approach. In later years when we stayed in Rosslare for the summer holidays I often came down on that train after a visit to town and its ponderous progress gave rise to much mischief. Teenagers then and young adults we often removed so many light bulbs in empty carriages that the train sidled into the station at Rosslare in near darkness. The poor old station-master who knew us all by sight if not by name, was often reduced to near apoplexy by our antics. How would he fare now, I wonder, if he had to deal with today's vandals. Our pranks were harmless and our mischief had no malevolence in it.

On our earlier jaunts with my mother, the half-hour journey seemed to take forever and then the trot down the station road until we got our first glimpse of the sea.

We could tell by its colour and motion if the swim was going to be idyllic or hard work. Either way we were in as soon as we could tear off our clothes. The days passed in a haze of sun and sea and all too soon it was time for the return journey. The house usually felt strange when we got back, somehow alien, and the sand in our hair and indeed our teeth after our picnic sandwiches held in sandy paws (and maybe even dropped a few times) felt out of place now and even tiresome. Worn out with the enormity of the whole adventure, we were too tired even to dream of our next foray or to begin to annoy our mother by starting the bargaining process again.

The first holiday we actually spent in Rosslare was when my mother rented a hut in the field next to Duggan's for two weeks in July. Now a hut could mean any number of things but in this case it was a converted Nissan hut – probably a relic of the "Emergency". It had bunk beds and a primus stove for cooking and all the water had to be carried from a pump in the farmyard, but for us children it was heaven. No more day-trips to the sea, we had joined the ranks of the elect and the beach was ours, morning, noon and night.

From early morning, when the seagulls sounded *Reveille* on the corrugated roof, until the evening tide lulled us to sleep again, it was action stations. We were within a stone's throw of the beach, just a short sandy stretch of lane and a few hillocks and there it was, no attic imaginings this time but the real McCoy; all our dreams wrapped in a wet blue blanket.

Each year we stayed longer and longer in our lovely summer place. We moved into Duggan's field and made our holiday home in a converted railway carriage from June to September. Memories of Rosslare come crowding into my mind: the scent of grass burned cream by summer sun and salt winds, or wet with dew or rain later in the year, the sand shimmering under a haze of heat, the water smooth as silk or throbbing and tossing fretfully, or glowing darkly out of reach of the moon on nights when we came back down over the hill for one last look to make sure it was still there, holding all the promise of unbounded pleasure in days ahead.

In their own way my mother and father loved and enjoyed the place as much as we did. The remembered image of my mother standing over the primus stove, cooking with the door open, watching the world outside as she worked, or cleaning out the saucepans with sea-sand, or crossing the field on Saturday evenings, returning from her weekly trip to town laden down with bags and parcels of "prog" as she called the provisions.

My father standing at the shore gazing out to the horizon in short sleeves, arms burned brown by the sun and wind, the two of them setting off to walk to the burrow and back each evening. All memories too deep for tears. The smell of the wild lupin, sun and heat, all the perfumes of a child's summer day, packed down and overflowing with the living only the young are capable of. The summers of our youth, given to us to make memories to carry us through the winters of our lives, so that when the light threatens to go out we can remember and go on.

Our games in Rosslare were more unmarked than the ones we played at home. Swimming took up most of our time, and rounders took on serious dimensions when played in a field. Teams were picked with care. I could always rely on being chosen for my brother's team because what I lacked in size and skill I made up for in cunning and speed. I was quick and devious. I suppose the fact that I was always small made it necessary for me to think and talk myself out of many a dangerous situation. Just as the fashion for one game or another had its own way of arriving and departing on the street the same rules seemed to apply during the holiday season. One week it was rounders and suddenly we would be trailing up to the tennis courts at the top of the village in the hope of getting a game or if we had the sixpence to hire a court for an hour we were in high glee. Travelling card games took over in the evenings and we played poker or whist into the small hours.

I still remember my disgust when my brother and some of the older boys started to show an interest in the young people's dances in the local hotel. The owner of this emporium had hit on a great fund-raising idea. By allowing the children into the dances for a few hours on Tuesday and Thursday nights before the serious punters arrived he could swell the coffers and be guaranteed enough cash to pay the band at least. Now I held out in my disdain for as long as I could, but eventually I had to join the dancers and I galloped around the floor of the Golf Hotel to the strains of "The Dark Town Strutters Ball" with the best of them. It was strange to see the lads transformed. Fellows whose only interest in the place up to now had been to harass the owner and the paying guests as much as possible (they had on one occasion stolen in, at night, and filled the holes in the clock golf course with gravel from the drive and then stood around nonchalantly next day watching the long-suffering players try to understand why their game had gone off to the extent that they could not get a single ball into a hole) were suddenly transformed into slick operators with sports coats and neatly-pressed pants and heads subdued by liberal applications of Brylcreem. Here they were trying to ignore us younger people as they tripped the light fantastic with the young girls from Dublin and Cork and tried to avoid the owner's eagle eye when it came to time for the children's dance to end.

I never suspected that one year I would find myself with pink skirt and stiff slip and Louis-heeled shoes joining in the ranks of the sophisticated, trying to look uninterested when the music started and the boys made their move to choose partners from the female ranks at the opposite end of the hall. But then everything comes into its season and even the worst tomboys must bow to the inevitable.

As the summer drew to a close we denied the facts as long as we could. The days were shorter in late August, the breeze a little cooler and one by one the few remaining families started to pack and move up to town. The tide was fuller now and it was possible to dive in right off the bank. We could not bear to tear ourselves away and when my mother started to gather our belongings together we made ourselves scarce. But the day came when we found ourselves back in Wexford and it was good to be back. Everything had indeed suffered a sea-change and there was much to rediscover. Old haunts to inspect, old games to be dusted off. How wise children are, they squeeze every drop from time when it arrives but then they drop the empty wineskin to make room in their hands for the new one, more anxious to taste this new wine than to savour that which has been drunk.

Chapter 10: Journeys

My mother's two brothers lived in Enniscorthy. The eldest, my uncle Johnny, had a house in the Shannon, under the shadow of Vinegar Hill. Johnny served his time in the forge and took over for a while when my grandfather died. He held on as long as there was work for a blacksmith in the Shannon but he saw his trade become obsolete while he was still a young man. Maybe this was what made him the silent type he was, for Johnny seldom spoke. He was fascinating, and like all my mother's family, something of an enigma. She claimed they were descendants of O'Doran the Irish Bard who warned one of the last great chiefs of the Irish clans that he was to be poisoned at a banquet he was attending and so saved his life. In my mind I suppose I always saw my uncle in the light of this story. He certainly was a figure from another age and steadfastly refused to recognise the twentieth century, probably because he saw moving with the times as more dangerous than most since it robbed him of his livelihood and his place in society. Not at all what one would expect a blacksmith to look like, he was a very small stocky man who always dressed in black. A quiet man but not dour, he could draw music from a stone, indeed I once heard him beat out a jig with a handful of stones by shaking them in his closed fist. Not only could he play most instruments, but he made his own banjos and guitars and carved out all sorts of whistles and pipes. His wife was a tall stately woman with a long plait of hair swinging down her back or pinned at the nape of her neck in a bun. She stood behind him as he sat and played and she accompanied him sometimes with a tambourine.

As a child I loved to travel to Enniscorthy to visit this gentle man and he never disappointed me. I can see him now sitting at the table in his home sprinkling salt over his potatoes because, like my grandfather, his favourite meal was potatoes and buttermilk. I remember tasting from the large mug beside his plate and spitting the contents half way across the room in disgust. Our taste was for more sophisticated fare than spuds and buttermilk. We would wait impatiently for Johnny to get down to the real business of the visit, but he could not be rushed. We had to content ourselves with turning the fan and watching the sparks rise from the big open wood fire or admiring his paintings over the fireplace, not painted on canvas or paper, but directly onto the wall itself. There was a particularly life-like white horse prancing on the chimney breast. I often wonder now what he used to paint it. He certainly had no elaborate brushes or tubes of paint. Soon we heard the spoons beginning to beat out a tune and the session would begin. The banjo, the accordion, the fiddle, once I heard him play a tune on a saw he had been using to cut firewood. Suddenly the silent man had found his voice, and what a voice. From jigs and hornpipes to plaintive laments, the music soared up and down and forward and back, as we sat listening or found ourselves leaping and jumping with it; wishing we were able to perform wonderful dances to express the emotions the music called up in us. Now and then the adults might take the floor and I remember my mother and her sisters once tackling a half set, but my mother's confidence failed her and she abandoned the effort after a short time.

We watched the hand-carved wooden dancing dolls gyrating on the end of a board while Johnny managed to make them perform a fair semblance of a hornpipe, by banging the end of the board with his fist. I was sure I could make the dolls dance and so I was presented with a board and a doll whom I was told was a Mr Adolf Hitler, a German person who was causing a bit of concern in the world at the time. Another character painted into a sailor's suit for some reason, and named Mussolini, accompanied him. I bore my trophies home and could hardly wait to see them perform but despite all my best efforts they refused to co-operate and seemed to have forgotten the steps. I consoled myself with the thought that they were foreigners anyhow.

As if to confirm my memories of him as being from another time altogether Johnny took us for our first and last trip in a pony and trap. He arrived at the house in the Faythe one lovely summer's day in a smart brown trap drawn by a lively little grey pony. I had never seen such a contraption close up and I was not too sure, as I was lifted up into it, if I really wanted to go. When the trap swayed with the pony's first steps I was even more unsure. But Johnny was in control and we made a lovely smooth turn and were off at a smart clip-clop across the Faythe and on our way. Our destination was the little valley called Eden Vale just outside the village of Castlebridge. I must have been very young, I know it was the longest journey I had ever taken from my home. I remember the heat and the strange, not unpleasant, pungent smells mingling – the pony and the creaking leather upholstery in the trap. I watched the little gate at the back with the black bolt that was shot when we were safely inside. I remember colours, white roads changing to dark blue tar, green trees soaring up and joining hands over our heads, penetrated by shafts of sunlight winking like golden stars. Most of all I remember the see-saw movements of the trap and the ponies' hooves beating out a rhythm, a music of their own as my uncle hummed an accompaniment.

I never travelled by pony and trap again, nor did I ever succeed in playing a musical instrument but they say such gifts skip a generation and my three sons all became accomplished musicians. We had many a session at our own fireside when they were growing up.

They always knew I loved to hear them play and often became impatient with my coaxing for more. Maybe I should have tried to explain to them about the house in the shadow of Vinegar Hill and the quiet man they would not remember. Johnny died as he stood in his garden one spring evening, when the eldest of them was still a baby, but as they say in the best songs, the music goes on.

The longest journey I made as a child and one that stands out in my memory, isolated from all journeys before or since, was a trip by car to Killarney. Our street boasted very few cars and we took no notice of the ones that stood here and there since we very seldom had any likelihood of getting a "scooch", as we called it, in any of them. My uncle was the proud owner of a Match Box, a Model T Ford. I was taken to Curracloe and back a few times in it but I was so prone to car sickness that the minute I entered a car my stomach started to misbehave. In spite of this when plans were drawn up for our epic trip, nobody mentioned the words "car sick" by mutual consent.

My father had a friend who drove a hackney car and he wanted to repay some favour to us. As we had never been to Killarney it was decided the whole family would be transported there and back in Christy's long black limousine. Killarney was a place I had heard John McCormack and Bing Crosby sing about. According to them it was the nearest place to heaven this side of the pearly gates and so beautiful even the angels visited regularly. I suppose in my mind it was up there with Disneyland, Hawaii and the Isles of the Blest. As the big day approached the whole family worked up a fine state of excitement and there was nearly as much preparation as the English army engaged in when getting ready for D-Day. My Aunt Nan was accompanying us and she was put in charge of provisions. As she had spent some time working in the kitchens of various hotels and eating houses, and had therefore a profound distrust of all such establishments, she decided we must transport all the food to be consumed on the day. For nearly a week before our own personal D-Day, my mother and herself cooked up a storm and we were in no doubt we would be able to eat the mountain of food they produced because we were on meagre rations all that week since they were too busy to make ordinary meals. Enough food to feed half the population of the town was prepared and packed into boxes and bags and these along with our plastic coats and umbrellas were carefully secreted away into the huge boot when the great day arrived and Christy drove up to our front door in the middle of the night. At least that's what it seemed like to us children as we were packed with equal care onto the shiny black seat. The stars were still in the sky over the Faythe and I could definitely see the faint outline of the moon over Kelly's pub.

I don't remember much about the journey except it revealed a whole new dimension of my father's personality. He sat in the front seat beside the driver and they carried on some fascinating conversations about the insides of cars, the state of the country and battles in countries where Mr Hitler had tried to march in Jack's boots.

Christy was a thin gangling man, well over six feet tall, had very little hair and because of his height he had a permanent stoop. He had a most peculiar laugh which started as a sort of cackle and ended up in a long- drawn-out wheeze and he had the sense of humour to match the laugh. Every time we passed females of any age or description on the roads and in the villages between Wexford and Kerry he wound down the windows and much to my father's embarrassment and our delight would roar, "Hello girls, do yez want boys?" After what seemed light years of winding roads and country towns with brief stops here and there to stretch our legs and perform any necessary ablutions, I was beginning to wonder if this was a penance or a pleasure, especially as I was on an enforced fast just in case the two pills I had swallowed before our dawn departure failed to work and my unmentionable trouble reared its ugly head. The arrival and time we spent in Killarney itself has faded into a grey memory of dreary discomfort, soggy fields and peering down through a murky haze of drizzle at a stretch of equally murky grey water which was one of the lakes of Killarney. I can still feel the mind-bending disappointment and the sense of disgust at our journey's end. So this was Killarney and I could not even comfort myself by over-eating as my mother's baleful eye was fixed on me with its warning of the wrath to come if I was sick on the return journey.

Over forty years elapsed before I really saw Killarney. Last year as I stood at Lady's View and looked out over the majestic Reeks to the sparkling blue waters of the lakes on a glorious June day, I knew they were right – Heaven reflects Killarney, and I forgave Count John and Bing Crosby.

Chapter 11: Autumn

When I was a child each season brought its own joy and autumn was rich with promise. We never saw it as the dying of the year and it brought no melancholic thoughts or feelings with it. By the time September evenings began to draw summer's shades we were nearly ready for indoor games and fireside stories.

But still there were fields to plunder and adventures to be had. Blackberry time was upon us and it was first come first served so we watched the ditches like hawks hovering over a chicken run. It was a skill to know just when to pick. Not too soon or the fruit was hard and sour, not too late or the rains could make them too soft and full of maggots. So at the right moment a flood of children with sweet cans or three-quart cans would forsake the streets and take to the fields and lanes around town. Dressed in our oldest and shabbiest clothes we attacked the brambles with gusto, risking life and limb or impalement to reach the juicy ones at the top. With purple faces and hands we straggled home in the evening with our booty and most mothers could be relied on to make a blackberry dumpling for the tea before the serious business of jam making got underway.

We knew all the good spots for picking and my father often came with us as he excelled at getting the juiciest and the ripest berries, something I think he was quite proud of. He had infinite patience and stood for hours picking away and carefully vetting each berry, discarding anything that looked even faintly suspicious and filling his can slowly. I am afraid we were not so careful and only wanted to see the cans full to the brim so we could lie down in the shade and rest. Crab jelly was another delicacy and we knew where to find crab apple trees and the wild damsons. Were we taught, I wonder, or was it passed down in some unspoken way? However we knew, we never ate anything harmful. We could chew the hawthorn leaves, bread and cheese, as it was called and suck the sour sals. We could use the haws as ammunition for our have spitter, a dangerous weapon made from a piece of bamboo or a dried stem of cow-parsley but we would never eat them. Sloes were used to brew wine. We only made this on one occasion and never tasted it because we buried it in the garden to ferment and forgot to mark the spot.

Evenings were chilly now and mothers came to the doors earlier to call us in from our games. We played under the street light outside our door and coaxed for another few minutes, promising not to wander away.

The street was friendly still, with the dark edges matching the black sky and the familiar lines softened by the light from the windows. We were reluctant to leave it and sat huddled on the edge of the path telling stories and daring one another to be afraid. I firmly believe that our Celtic souls have an affinity with autumn and I strongly suspect there was enough of the pagan in us when we were young to be closer to the real Creator of our Universe than when we had been put through the system. Because we instinctively knew our own littleness and how defenceless we really were, we accepted the idea of being protected and watched over. Our parents were there for the obvious needs but we were close enough to the heart of things, to the breath of the earth, to know there was something more.

We knew too that it was good and loving. Not with a soft or sentimental love but with a hardness that had at its core more tenderness than we could really grasp. A child can lie on the earth and know without knowing. There is still enough of the unformed there to communicate without words getting in the way. I know because all the pain and seeking in my own life only brought me back to the knowledge I had when I lay on the black rich earth of the potato drills, hidden by the foliage, listening. The black earth held me, hid me and protected me and the white flowering stalks joined the conspiracy and covered me. But the conspirator was more than the clay and the foliage, and the oneness I felt needed no explanation.

So on autumn nights when darkness held hands all around the edges of the Faythe we sensed we were at the source of something mystical, caught between two worlds and though we always turned our backs on the night eventually, and ran for the shelter of the familiar hall-doors, we flirted a little with the shadows and felt that delicious feeling of promise, of being poised on the brink.

Our stories were all of headless horsemen and strange lights appearing in the fields, of banshee and fairy people and sightings of the dead. We had as yet no one of our own to mourn, so the dead were talked of in the same breath as hobgoblins and ghosts. I remember one evening we paraded across the street, banded close together for courage, to attend the wake of an old woman who had just died. It was the first time I saw a corpse and I was sorely disappointed. I don't know what I expected, but the figure laid out in black with waxy face and rosary-entwined hands bore a close resemblance to the little Saint in the Friary and my mother had assured me he was only a statue. The candles flickering in the room and the faces of the mourners kneeling around the bed and the strange odour of death compensated a little for our disappointment. We mooched back across the Faythe, seriously deflated and wondering again about the adult world where such events were made so much of.

There was much to be enjoyed in autumn. The huge rifts of fallen leaves down along the Folly Hill occupied many an evening. We waded through them in our wellington boots and looked for buried treasure. Lovely shiny brown chestnuts that could be threaded on twine for necklaces or used for games of conkers, hazelnuts and windmills, as we called the sycamore seeds – another generation of children would call them helicopters but that word was still not in our vocabulary.

Then there were the skies. The summer colours are surely sucked up from the earth by the skies of autumn.

How often I stood at the end of the Folly Hill and looked up with wonder at a November sky before sunset. At that time I had no name for, or understanding of the emotions that surged through me, just a nameless longing to be part of the splendour. I found that if I looked long enough and with enough intensity I could indeed feel as if I were part of this great rolling golden-scarlet grandeur. When, as an adult, I discovered William Blake and read his searing, agonising words, I realised what I had experienced was God's way of drawing greatness from the clay that we are. He does this by calling us to re-create, with Him, some of the beauty He tantalises us with glimpses of, in things like autumn skies.

But such existential moments were balanced off with the excitement of banging the paint off our neighbours front doors with cabbage stumps on cabbage stump night. This was the name we had for Halloween. You had really gained your spurs when you were allowed to go out with the older boys and girls and do the rounds on this special night. We never collected anything, only wreaked havoc on the doors with our strange missives. I don't know what the origins of the custom were but we understood the banging on the door was meant to strike terror into the people in the house thinking that the dead were trying to gain entry. We must have believed that the dead were a noisy lot. In my day this was a harmless enough occupation but I believe it got out of hand in later years and had to be stopped.

Cabbage stump night or dip night was high on our calendar of events and my father really entered into the spirit of things though my mother was not too happy about the ensuing mess. A tin bath of water was placed in the middle of the room when we children returned from our noisy annunciation of the arrival of the dead.

Apples and nuts were floated in the water and for the really daring divers a shiny sixpence was thrown in and lay winking and beckoning on the bottom of the tub.

We rolled up our sleeves and taking deep breaths would dip our faces into the icy water only to come up spluttering and gasping and frustrated. Hands had to grasp the edge of the tin bath firmly and could not be used in any way to help the bobbing apples into the open mouths of the half drowned and frenzied dippers.

When my father reckoned we had had enough, the water was mopped up and he had another fiendish torture for us. This time a string was suspended from the ceiling with an apple swinging on the end of it. Our hands were tied behind us and the object of the exercise was to grasp the swinging apple with the teeth. If you could hold onto it, it was yours. This game usually ended in temper tantrums and tears so the spoils had to be divided and we tried something gentler. We scrabbled blindfolded, for saucers of clay, or water, or rosary beads, or ring, with the obvious connotations.

Lashings of tea or cocoa and barm brack had to be consumed on top of all the apples and nuts. No wonder we had strange dreams on Halloween Night.

As autumn wore on and the nights grew longer we had to reluctantly leave our outdoor pursuits. We fought the elements bravely and ignored the rain as much as we could. But mothers were inclined to fret that wet and bedraggled children would catch cold easily. After all, we were wartime children and orange juice and vitamins were in short supply. Boils and chilblains now began to show head in earnest and the smell of Zambuc and other ointments and lotions fought with the odour of incense and sanctity in the churches at the October devotions and the Sunday masses.

I was swathed in wool for the cold weather. The hated woollen vest made its comeback and I endured its itching and chafing because I was led to believe without it I would never see another spring. Fires were lit and hot bottles were put into our beds on really cold nights.

My mother made valiant efforts to say the rosary but we were reluctant prayers, egged on in our rebellion by my father, whose lack of interest in all religious practices was periodically decried. We were avid readers, soon graduating from comics to books and there was very little complaint about the long dark nights. We soon had our noses stuck in some book or other as my mother complained about our inactivity. Far from having to be encouraged to read, she gave us long lectures, complete with dire warnings on the ills that might befall the bookworm. Looking back now I wonder did she miss our company around the house or was she wise enough to apply the psychology of the forbidden fruit tasting sweeter. Anyhow we could never be separated from our beloved books – perhaps there was method in her madness.

Chapter 12: School

When my older brother was five he went to school. This left me with large problems because we had never been separated and I could not put up with the situation so I decided to follow him. I must have created some mighty scenes because, eventually, my mother gave in and trotted me up to the gates of the St John of God school at the top of the Faythe even though I was just two and a half years old.

She told me she was met by an irate Reverend Mother who told her to take me home as the nuns were not running a kindergarten. However, I persisted and instead of crying because I had to go to school I cried because they would not have me. Eventually the nuns relented and I was allowed into the babies' room where I stayed for two years happy in the knowledge that my brother was just up the hall.

I remember the rocking-horse but then so does everyone who passed through the hallowed portals of the Faythe school. This gallant wooden horse welcomed every baby who was lucky enough to begin his or her school days with Sr Mary John, the jolly little apple-cheeked nun who has survived to this very day in spite of the best efforts of successive generations of Wexford children.

Unlike a great many of my generations I have no bad memories of my school days. I loved every day I spent there, maybe because it was so hard for me to gain entrance in the first place. I never had difficulty learning. I had a quick mind and, of course, I soon found favour with the nuns though we had our fair share of rows. It was at school I first discovered that some people had a much harder life than I had. I sat beside girls who had no winter clothes, no coats, no wellington boots, girls who were cold and thin and hungry. At the end of the school yard was the red shed where the nuns brewed cocoa at lunch-time and distributed thick slices of bread and jam and on special occasions currant buns. I always wanted to go to the red shed for my lunch instead of going home and I could never understand the disdain of some of my contemporaries for the girls who ate there. My mother tried to explain the complexities of the situation to me but I still wanted to sit on the wooden forms and drink cocoa out of a tin mug and eat thick bread and jam from the linoleum-covered tables.

Then too there was a puzzling availability of black babies. I saved up my pennies carefully and saw them all disappear into the voluminous skirts of Sr Assumpta, but all I got for my efforts were a few hairy chocolate sweets of uncertain vintage dredged out of the same pockets, along with a holy picture of St Philomena or Marie Goretti, both long-forgotten saints of my youth. No matter how many pennies I brought the black baby never materialised. I was assured that I owned one all right, out in the depths of darkest Africa. We were also told that every baby we bought was given our name and so I can assume that there are legions of middle-aged African ladies today sporting the unlikely name of Ann Veronica Mary. We learned new games in the school yard and here segregation was strictly enforced. We girls skipped with ropes or walked around in rings with hands joined chanting long rigmaroles with very derogatory rhymes about certain persons who were out of favour for one reason or another. There were bullies too, girls who pulled ribbons off our hair and pinched and punched slyly and one girl whose mother, the local harridan, was much feared by all and sundry. She had only to threaten to tell tales at home and we were all running with bribes to buy her silence. I once decided to take the law into my own hands and gave her a severe trouncing only to be faced by my mother's rage when I got home. The dreaded one had descended the length of the Faythe, rapped on our door and attacked my poor mother with gusto. My father who always took my side, was dragged into the argument when he arrived home. After all, my mother insisted, the boys had never caused anyone to come to our door in anger, it would take me to do that, unruly wretch that I was.

As I got older and entered the senior classes I think I began to develop a split personality. At school I was the good girl, quiet and studious but underneath the wildness was still there. I often spent long drowsy afternoons looking longingly out of the windows over the fields to Maiden Tower and the rocks beyond. The smell of new books and the pristine whiteness of the first pages of a brand new copybook had to fight hard to hold my spirit captive. Maybe I had some inkling then of what I was giving up in the pursuit of learning. I think I was too eager a student, I did not temper my enjoyment of learning, book-learning that is, with learning the art of living and growing in other ways. I could easily earn the praise I longed for both at home and in school, learning came easily but involved much solitude. I gave up my childhood too easily and too soon.

One of my fondest memories of school during the middle years is of the girls I came to know. Here were girls from all over the town and the countryside and from various backgrounds. But my dearest friend, the one I gave my heart to completely, was a girl from the top of the Faythe. She was a grave little girl with glasses and a long plait of thick blond hair hanging down her back and we must have been like chalk and cheese. From the moment we were seated together in the same desk in high babies we became inseparable.

Who can explain the chemistry between young children that solders them together sometimes for life? Phil and I became like two halves of the same coin and our names were linked for the rest of our school days. Her parents were stricter than mine and she had a much more sheltered existence before I came on the scene. But I was soon enticing her down my neck of the woods. we went to the May devotions arm in arm and back again for the Rosary in October. We set to work coaxing her mother to allow Phil to go to the Saturday matinee and when we were a little older we both fell in love with a very young Rock Hudson. Phil had relations in America who sent her movie magazines and we pored over these believing everything written about the Hollywood stars. She and I were small for our age and shared the disgrace of being sent to the *Feis* and the annual Plain Chant competitions with the younger children in the lower classes who needed extra singers, though Phil was no singer. She was the first to admit that she sounded more like a crow than a lark.

We were together through our school days and right up to the time her family went to America when we were about twelve years old. Emigration had only been a word to me until the day Phil and her family left for Cobh and the ship to the USA. It was my first experience of real loss and I think the first time my heart broke. Happily, our friendship survived the distance and the years and we still manage to meet, now and then, when she comes back to visit the old haunts.

After a few minutes conversation the time in-between vanishes like the illusion it is and we are two little girls again, running in spirit, hand and hand down the Faythe.

Chapter 13: Christmas

Everything is relative and yet I cannot help but wonder if children today can possibly enjoy or savour anything as much as we did when we were young. In our modern day society when every day seems to be Christmas for so many youngsters, when their world is chock-a-block with toys and possessions of all sorts, it is hard to imagine a child appreciating or looking forward with longing and excitement. Maybe their longings and excitements are as fierce as ours were, but for different things.

I suppose I would be pilloried by the masses, certainly by the intelligentsia, for looking back with such nostalgia to a time when the horn of plenty was far more lightweight than it is today. Maybe I could be excused on the grounds that people of my age look at the past through rose-coloured glasses because we are seeing our youth. Whatever the reason I still insist that Christmas worked when I was a child. The whole concept of joy being born to the world really happened for us, it was the high point of our lives, it was magic.

There were no advertising jingles to put us on our guard in October, no lights on Christmas trees to be switched on in November, but when the annuals arrived in Bucklands book shop the news spread like wildfire. Every child in the Faythe caught the scent and like bloodhounds we were off to see for ourselves. *The Beano*, the *Dandy*, *Boys' Own*, *Film and Radio Fun*, their appearance was as reliable as the leaves in springtime and just as exciting. They had a feel and a smell all of their own and no child would really want to do more than gaze at this early stage because the touching and opening were sacred to Christmas morning itself. The next shrine to be visited was Georgie Bridge's shop where the toys were on display. Meccano sets bigger and better than last year's and dolls that would take your breath away, most of the mothers in the town had been paying visits here for many weeks past and the goods would be finally paid for and collected on Christmas Eve itself.

We had the added excitement every year of collecting a large box from the old coach yard at White's Hotel where the Dublin bus arrived. Aunt Nan never failed us and the box disgorged its wonderful contents on to our floor, whipping the excitement up to fever pitch, even though we could only guess at what the carefully wrapped parcels and smaller boxes inside contained.

Every family had its rituals which were carefully observed. In our house my father worked until lunchtime on Christmas Eve and we watched and waited anxiously for his appearance at the top of Castle Hill Street. He ate his lunch and performed his ablutions, donning his good clothes in slow-motion, or so it appeared to us as we waited in nail-biting excitement for the show to get on the road. When he at last signalled his willingness to depart we were off before him across the Faythe and down into the heart of Christmas Eve Wexford, where most of our contemporaries were already thronging the streets and shops. This was my father's finest hour and he loved it. He paraded his family in slow procession down to his sister's shop, in North Main Street. His brother and sisters were also assembled there and because this was the season of goodwill my mother acquiesced without a murmur. Here was such an air of largesse that we children knew we were on to a good thing and sure enough our uncle usually started the ball rolling by encouraging us to choose something for ourselves. So we had a bar of chocolate or a bottle of lemonade to begin the festivities. I remember the year my young brother when pressed to make his choice, picked out a box of Black Magic chocolates and what could the uncle do but buy them or lose face in front of the whole family. We were left gasping at his audacity and filled with envy at his good fortune.

Our journey back up the town was slow. Parcels were collected and marvellously shaped packages called for at various shops. By the time we arrived back at the Faythe we were drunk with excitement and longing, but we had one more port of call and that was to our cousins' house at the corner. Here my aunt would be up to her elbows in breadcrumbs while a large turkey with gaping orifices and legs in the air waited for her ministries and iced cakes and puddings in white bowls stood side by side on the press. All work was laid aside and tea was taken, no food for the adults though for this was the time when Christmas Eve was a day of fast which was observed until midnight.

For the people of Wexford in those times Midnight Mass in the Friary signalled the beginning of the Feast of Christmas and every child longed to be old enough to attend. People who belonged to the Third Order of St Francis were given tickets and these were precious because the Friary was so packed it was nearly impossible to get a seat without one. The first time I was there I sat in the transept with my father and mother and my older brother and fought the tiredness and sleep. The beauty of the ceremony held me up, the three priests in golden robes exultantly intoning the words of the Latin Mass, flowers and candles and the wafting incense, the choir singing the ancient beautiful Franciscan hymn, *Jesu Bambino*, all leading up to the unveiling of the crib with the lifelike figures and the Christ-child lying like a real baby in the straw of the manger. Walking home through the frosty night, watching the star-laden sky over the town it was easy to believe in Peace on Earth, goodwill to men.

The single event that caused most excitement in our house when we were young was the arrival of Santa Claus on Christmas Eve.

The only night in the year we did not have to be coaxed to bed early, indeed we watched the clock from about six onwards and the hands seemed to crawl so slowly towards an hour when we could decently withdraw without losing too much face. Then the long wait for the magic arrival began. Unfortunately the one thing necessary to ensure the happening was that all good children were fast asleep. Sleep, when pursued, always proves to be a most elusive quarry. So we lay tossing and turning for hours, listening to every creak and groan as the old house settled for the night.

Our letters had been written and left on the ledge at the side of the chimney to be collected by the fairy servants and they were always taken promptly because when we reached our hands up into the sooty recesses the morning after carefully leaving them in place, the post was always gone. So now we waited in the darkness and willed ourselves asleep while the excitement nearly choked us with the thought of goodies to come. When we had given up all hope of lasting the pace, suddenly the impossible had happened.

We woke with a start, we must have slept because there was a subtle change. The darkness had lightened a little, the stillness had deepened, and yes, the weight was here at the end of the bed, the smell of the new books mixed with the scent of oranges and chocolate. The scrabbling, sniffing and touching began, no handy bedside lamps to cut short the anticipation as we hugged our treasures and we explored the shapes and feel of our booty to make sure what we asked for had arrived.

Who can ever forget the wonder of Christmas morning? Even as we grew up a little and began to doubt the existence of Santa, we were willing to believe again to prolong the magic of that special night. Poised on the threshold of another world holding out so much more promise, we did not want to pay the price demanded of us so we delayed the pass over as long as we could. It was not simply for what we got, because our presents would arrive anyhow but instinctively we knew that when we took the step it would be a giant one which would take us out of one world and into another and the doors that swung closed behind us would never ever open again.

There are people who argue that it is wrong to let children believe and that the inevitable disillusionment is too cruel. I say let Father Christmas live as long as he can along with all that is magical and innocent about childhood itself. When it has to pass let it be not a disillusionment but a transition into something deeper, a knowledge and belief in the spirit that moves us to want to give joy to others, especially children. Maybe the venerable old gentleman is a cover-up for the dream of love that lives deep down in even the most disillusioned amongst us.

We spent one Christmas in Dublin, my mother, my brother and myself. I was very young and I don't know why my father was not with us. It was the first time I ever saw my mother in tears and I know I was amazed. I had never associated my mother with the act of crying. I imagined she was the centre where all power lodged and everything began and ended. To see her reduced to such a state confused me so much I decided to ignore it. Anyhow my very real worry was whether Santa Claus knew where we were. The ritualistic letter writing had been disrupted. I found it hard to believe Aunt Nan would really post our letters and I was highly sceptical when they disappeared into her famous black bag. On Christmas morning I was relieved to find that the magic had happened. As I sat up in bed reading my *Gussy Goose* annual and risking a sneak preview of my box of *Silver Lining* chocolates my world was still intact and nothing else mattered.

Maybe my father and mother were going through a bad patch, I know it was at this time my mother was trying to persuade him to emigrate to England. This would have been anathema to my father who was a Wexford man to the core.

We were driven back in style in a large black limousine belonging to my father's employer. The driver stopped outside the town at a particular spot where one can glimpse the lights of Wexford for the first time. The lights twinkling like little stars in the distant darkness filled me with a great happiness. I still love to reach that spot on the Wexford Road and look out for the glowing lights, now much bigger and brighter. The experience is akin to the softening around the heart one feels when the first evening star appears at the end of a good day.

When daylight exposed the house in the Faythe in all its pristine splendour we saw that my father had painted the doors and windows and every piece of exposed wood in the building a bright shade of pink. Whether this was done to alleviate the boredom when we were away or in an effort to welcome us home I do not know. My mother swallowed her horror and waited a decent interval before covering the

offending pink surfaces with something a little more subtle.
We were all happy to be home.

Chapter 14: Aunt Nan

"**M**ind that auld fellow, he might spit on you" That was my Aunt Nan in full flight and the auld fellow in question was the poet Paddy Kavanagh.

We children gave him a wide berth as he stood, one-legged like a stork, outside Mooney's pub on the corner of Baggot Street and Mespil Road. Of course Paddy was not a famous poet in those days nor was he particularly old, but he was fairly grumpy and he would never win a prize for his mannerly behaviour. My Aunt Nan would have been an able contender in any bout with the poet. She would, as my mother used to say, give him or any other man a run for his money. Maybe Paddy was able to size her up because he never did spit on us, even if he heard her derogatory remarks as we passed, his growling undertones only got a little more insistent.

If I had not had an Aunt Nan I would have had to invent her, because all stories have to have a fairy godmother and she was ours. My mother's oldest sister, she left home to go skivvying in Dublin, like so many a young country girl, in the early 1900s. When I knew her she had become a cook and more Dublin than the Dubliners themselves. She lived in two rooms in Percy Place, a small street near the canal, not far from Baggot Street and every time we could get away from home on any pretext, we made for her welcoming presence.

Her Dublin became our Dublin and we adjusted to it as easily as a duck to water. We were as happy sitting on the steps in Percy Place with the local children or roaming the surrounding streets and lanes as we were in Wexford. Our only grouse, everyone in Dublin was convinced we came from the country. As most of the people we mixed with had never been to Dun Laoghaire, they shared Brendan Behan's belief that everything outside Tallaght was bog, so we gave up trying to tell them about our home town.

We walked everywhere in those days and a ride on a bus was a special treat. Walking through Dublin with Aunt Nan was pure pleasure and I trailed happily after her so often I became familiar with the city at a young age. Walking with her was an education you could never get in a schoolroom. I put my finger into the bullet holes in the Custom House, I saw the street and alleyways where the "Big Fellow" cycled on a messenger boy's bike and waved at the British soldiers as he passed them by. Michael Collins was the one and only man I ever heard her praise. When she spoke his name her voice softened and the stories she told about him she said like prayers.

We knew how to coax the information from her. All we had to do was throw in some remark from our teacher or school book and she was off. Her knowledge was not tinged with politics, nor was she. She had a sublime disregard for all politicians living and dead, but she had lived through those times with the poor people of Dublin. She was there when history was being made. Michael Collins was the darling of the young country girls who lived and worked in the city. One of their own to be looked after, and some say without the help of those young girls, of whom Aunt Nan was one, he would never have escaped capture. "Then to be shot by his own," the tears would stand in her eyes and we looked in amazement and wondered about this man whose memory could make our tough aunt cry after all those years. But he was the only man who could touch her heart. Her father, or my father, or anyone else's father, was dismissed with a loud disdainful sniff and she boasted about all the proposals of marriage she had refused. Men were nothing but nuisance, she informed us on many an occasion and I suppose she only excluded my brothers from this rule on the grounds that they were underage.

When we passed Boland's Mill and the bridge over the canal at the end of Percy Place we were given a colourful account of De Valera's part in the battle. I could never understand why she had such contempt for him because he used his American citizenship to escape being shot. I thought it was a bit like the cavalry to the rescue in all the best westerns. Of course I never said so because in her view the Big Fellow was the good guy and the Long Fellow was definitely the bad guy and I tried never to disagree on any subject dear to Aunt Nan's heart.

When we stayed with our aunt we shared more than her home. Her neighbours and friends became our adopted community. We entered fully into the life of the poorer people of Dublin at that time and they were the "heart of the rowl". Their poverty was more pervasive than that of their country cousins, accentuated as it was by the concrete surroundings and the crumbling old houses and flats they occupied. We saw the people and the places through her eyes and she loved them.

Upstairs in her building lived a typical Dublin family, father, mother and six children all higgledy-piggledy together in two rooms with a sink on the landing outside their door and a toilet in the backyard for the use of all the inhabitants of the house. The mother was a little round woman with a rich Dublin accent who always addressed my aunt formally as Miss Doran. Her husband was a tiny little man, meek as a lamb when sober but a roaring lion when possessed by the demon drink. Their six children were our constant companions and though they were tough and streetwise they were kindly children and let their "country cousins" tag along.

Mr and Mrs Black had their share of rows but the family for all their hardships were happy and rumbustious. She never said a bad word about her husband even when Aunt Nan lambasted him to her after a particularly noisy night. She always made some excuse for him, even after he was eventually carted away by two men in white coats in the middle of a drunken fit. On the way out the hall he managed to kick in Aunt Nan's door and appeal to her for help. Far from being frightened we thought it was all very exciting and could hardly wait to discuss it with his long-suffering family. He soon returned to the flat upstairs and it was not long before himself and the Mrs were setting off arm in arm for their weekly night out. I often think now of the zest for life those inner city people had and how they managed not only to survive but to knock so much enjoyment out of life in spite of their circumstances.

We, for our part, saw no reason to feel anything only envy for the young Blacks. They were free to wander the streets and to swim in the canal when summer came, something we were never allowed to do. When they came home covered in blood, or bruises, or both, their mother never got angry with them. She just grabbed her coat and ran with them to the casualty department of Baggot Street Hospital. Even the day Willy was dragged half-drowned from the canal and rushed off by ambulance, she kept her head and said very little. We could only put it down to the fact that there were so many of them, she would not miss one or two. We wished we had more brothers and sisters, thinking if we had we could escape my mother's eagle eye now and then and have more scope for our obvious talents.

Summer days in Dublin were spent down in Herbert Park fishing for minnows in the lake, or tearing around the grassy slopes until we trooped back home at evening hot and thirsty. There was a house on the way where we bought large sugar bags full of apples for a halfpenny, or a small farthing bag. We were amazed at this good fortune because the farthing had already disappeared in Wexford and the halfpenny was the smallest negotiable coin. After tea we congregated on the steps of a house down the street where a girl called Maureen lived. Maureen's mother worked as an usherette in the Theatre Royal so she was at work most nights and we felt it our duty to keep Maureen company for as long as we could. We learned all the Dublin games and songs and heard some great ghost stories. We absorbed the colour and taste of the city the very best way, at its roots.

The Dublin I knew then was a little jewel of a city where poets mused on street corners and writers lay in the grass amongst the wild flowers on the banks of the canal. Where Behan could sleep it off on the middle of Mount Street with his coat under his head for a pillow, where a Theatre was closed for putting on a pagan play, where we kids ran three times around the Pepper Canister in order to see the Devil appear on top. A country city where you could walk at night in safety and where you kept the Pillar in your sights if you were not too sure of the way. Where Sandymount Strand was heaven for the hot dusty children and mothers could get a kettle of boiling water to make tea for tuppence.

James Joyce's shadow was still warm on Howth Hill and a tram took you up and back, and the smell of the buses passing by was perfume in the nostrils of two kids from the country.

All the restraints of our upbringing relaxed in Aunt Nan's world. This was a woman who had definitely cut all the shackles and become a free spirit. When we went to the chipper on Mespil Road of an evening, she was the one who banged the door knockers and ran all the way home and we were her reluctant accomplices. Her style was all in her bearing, because she put comfort before dress sense every time. Her motto was, "if it is uncomfortable cut a hole in it," and her many-layered look owed nothing to the fashion of the time. She had no regard for the petty rules and regulations and made her way blithely through life with freedom.

I suppose the story that best describes Aunt Nan was how she came to have a lodger in later years. When proceeding home along Baggot Street one evening she came upon an old lady sitting on the street at a bus stop clutching a couple of plastic bags. Stopping for a chat she discovered that the woman was homeless, having just been evicted from her flat. She was a little bird-like person who had obviously seen better days. Not one to hesitate Aunt Nan promptly invited her home and ensconced her in one of her two rooms. Here Miss Satelle, that was the bag lady's name, lived out the rest of her days rent-free. At an advanced age she went into hospital where Aunt Nan visited her every Sunday, bringing some choice little titbit to eat until she eventually died.

My aunt never knew very much about the old lady except her father had been a fencing instructor from France and she had had quite a privileged childhood. Far from being grateful she was a cantankerous old soul and an uneasy truce existed between the two of them.

Aunt Nan always referred to her as "that old biddy" but it never occurred to her to get rid of her. She had taken her in because she had nowhere to go, not with any idea of doing good works or anything "mauzy" like that. My aunt had a dread of being "mauzy", a word she coined herself which was self-explanatory.

One by one we migrated to Dublin. My brother to the University, me to work, my younger brother in his turn. We all lived with Aunt Nan. We graduated to a flat in Mount Street and we moved up in the world but Aunt Nan never changed. She disappeared down Moore Street every Saturday morning with a large black bag and haggled with the traders as was her wont. She came back bearing her booty and turned it into meals fit to lay before a king. She fed the multitudes. All the relations up for the match, all our friends and acquaintance were welcome.

She went to Terenure to babysit for a Jewish family she met somewhere and died quietly in their front room. They found her on the sofa with a smile on her face and were loath to part with her even in death. But the powers that be insisted she could not remain to be waked in a Jewish household, so she was brought to the morgue in Baggot Street hospital and laid out on a slab. I was miles away looking after my own small son. At the exact time she died I was overcome with feelings of intense sadness and I cried long and hard. I like to think I was in her thoughts at the end and her love was strong enough to reach out and touch me.

Chapter 15: Troubled Times

My grandfather, my mother's father, was one of the last blacksmiths in our part of the country. I don't know if it was the heat of the forge that gave him a great thirst, but he could sink pints with the best of them. My mother both amused and confused us when she spoke about him because it was clear to us children she thoroughly disliked him. My own father was such a gentle man we could not understand this and felt there must be some mistake. But the facts were there. When my mother talked about him it was as if he was a stranger she had been unfortunate enough to know when she was young. We questioned her carefully and listened for some change in the stories or in her tone of voice. There was a disquieting consistency in her answers and so we built up a picture of the man over the years. He led his family a merry dance, if you could use that expression about a man who constantly came home drunk and raised hell. I never knew my grandmother, she died when my mother was quite young, but according to all accounts she was a quiet long-suffering soul who had never seen her husband until she met him at the altar at the age of sixteen. It was a "made match".

Yet in between the bad bits we gleaned information that build up a slightly different picture or maybe lightened it a little and added some softness and shading here and there.

We never tired of hearing the story about my grandfather's run-in with the devil himself.

How one night when he was returning home along a country lane he heard a strange clanking sound behind him and even though he stopped and looked all around, peering into the darkness, he saw nothing. Every time he set off the clanking started up. If he hurried the noise kept pace, if he slowed down so did his invisible companion. At last totally unnerved and sweating he set off at a gallop convinced that old Nick himself had come to take him. No doubt he had plenty on his conscience to make him think the worst. He arrived at the end of the lane only to be met at the gate of the top field by a large billy-goat who had broken away from where he was tethered and was dragging his chain after him. Poor old Billy had accompanied poor old Granda on the other side of the ditch listening anxiously to the man's footsteps and looking for a bit of company on a dark night.

As children we would coax my mother to tell us this tale or to recount how her father was allowed safe passage during the Troubles by boxing clever and never letting anyone know where he stood. When the Free Staters shouted, "Halt, who goes there, Friend or Foe?" and he called out his name they called back, "Pass on", and the same thing happened with the opposition. I suppose a blacksmith was a valuable ally in those days when horses were still useful for a quick getaway.

All our surmising about this dark figure came to a head when my mother announced out of the blue that her father was coming to visit us. I don't know what the background to the visit was as up to now he had lived with my uncle and we seldom saw him except on rare visits to my uncle's home. I remember once visiting him in the forge in the Shannon. He was a commanding figure tall and lean with his leather apron tied around him as he sweated over the glowing coals. The smell of the heat and the sparks flying off the red-hot iron, the sizzling when it was plunged into the cold water and the smell of scorched hooves all mingle in my mind when I think of that day. I don't know if it was during that visit that he burned through his arm when a red-hot metal bar slipped, or if I was told about it later. When the accident happened he reached for a bottle of whiskey and poured some of it over the wound, wrapped his shirt around his arm, drank the rest of the whiskey and continued working until darkness fell.

The haunted room at the top of the stairs was made ready and we became very excited at the thought of our expected guest. In appearance he turned out to be a frail old eighty-year-old, tall still but with a cane to help him walk. But if we were hoping for fireworks we were not disappointed for age had not wrought a miraculous conversion. He began almost immediately to torment my mother, tease us until we made ourselves scarce and wage warfare against the dog. The dog was the first to crack. A fine pure-bred Kerry Blue he was of a fairly nervous disposition and thoroughly ruined by all and sundry so he was not able for my grandfather's guerilla tactics. One day when we arrived from school we were told the dog was gone and that was that. Strike one against our new lodger.

It soon became obvious my mother was not exactly happy with the situation. Little things that made us laugh, she did not find amusing. When she asked if he wanted salt during meals for instance, he would say "No", she would say "No what?" and he would answer, "No salt", winking slyly at us. Our manners at table and in general, never over-robust, began to become distinctly unhealthy. Things limped along unsteadily until one night the crunch came when he fell off the wagon and arrived home roaring drunk. Even at his advanced age he could kick up quite a rumpus and no one was amused. We knew the end had come and sure enough the old gentleman was sent packing that weekend and the house settled back into its teetotal state again with heartfelt sighs of relief from one and all.

My grandfather had been warned to give up the drink at sixty years of age because his heart could not stand the pace. He disregarded the advice and died at eighty-four after drinking two Baby Powers. I would say off-hand he died happy.

Because Wexford is situated right on the coast, the Second World War impinged on our lives quite a bit. Apart from the scarcity of food and fuel during the Emergency there were many lives lost at sea and nearly every family was left to mourn some relative in England.

Then there was the bombing in Campile and at Tuskar Light House. My father worked at the Pier in Rosslare Harbour at that time and he was there when the bodies were brought in. I remember his distress on one occasion when he returned, in the morning, after helping to recover the bodies from the wreckage of a German Aircraft.

I was too young to understand anything of the horror the world was plunged into in the war years but I do recall little things, like seeing my mother making "logs" for the fire by filling sugar bags with wet slack and trying to make a fire with soggy lumps of turf and on one occasion using an old pair of shoes to get the blaze going.

How could I forget the time the word spread like wildfire up the Faythe that there was chocolate on sale down town in one of the chemist shops? Now, sweets of any description were at a premium so we were off like hounds on the scent of a hare. Some of the older children managed to get their hands on the "chocolate" and we tore into it even though it had a rather peculiar taste. In the wee small hours of the morning households were thrown into a panic by the onset of one of the worst cases of diarrhoea ever known in the street. Only the children were affected and the mystery was solved when the wrapping paper was found and the chocolate turned out to have been a particularly lethal laxative which taken even in minute quantities was guaranteed to move mountains. The children of the Faythe were very wary of chocolate for a long time.

My father's cousin, a young girl who had gone to England, to work, had married an Englishman and subsequently moved to Germany before the war, was lost and for years the family had Masses offered for the repose of her soul. Once my father showed me her photo. Here he was, a handsome young daredevil, looking a bit like Rudolph Valentine, with hair sleeked back, dressed to the nines in a dark suit and waistcoat, arms around a lovely young girl who was smiling up at him. He told me they had been engaged but because they were first cousins the family had frowned on the romance and sent her to England to live with an aunt. At the time it meant very little to me, even though it was rather strange to see my father in a romantic light. However, I was to remember that little snapshot and it took on a strange poignancy for me many years later.

One day in the early Sixties, when I was in Wexford on holidays with my husband and children, my father came home in a state of high excitement. He told us Mary, his cousin, had returned from the dead and was on a visit to the family home place outside the town. He asked my husband and I if we would come with him to see her and we drove down together. As we approached the village of Ballymitty we saw a lone woman walking along the road ahead and my father said, "That's Mary." We stopped the car and he got out and approached her. She turned to meet him and without a word, it seemed to me, they walked off together. We drove on to the cottage and waited with the other relations who had gathered to welcome the lost sheep. We were introduced to her husband who was Lebanese and her son, a tall handsome young man who was at university in England. We spent the evening in their company and Mary turned out to be quite a cultured woman who bore little or no resemblance to the laughing young girl in my father's faded photo.

Not surprising when one heard the story of the missing years. Apparently she was one of the few survivors of the bombing of Dresden, when her first husband perished with all the other victims on that terrible night. She was sent to a camp in North Africa where she made bullets for Rommel's desert troops and was still alive when the allied liberation took place. She stayed in Libya and was nursing in a hospital there when she met and married a doctor and made a new life for herself. I don't know what motivated her to return after so many years. Maybe the trauma of her wartime suffering had lessened enough to allow her to make contact with a previous life that must have seemed like a dream, or maybe she had things to say to those that remained at home, including my father.

It must be a tribute to the generation that went before us that we remember so little of the horror of the times we were born into and that what we recall most of all is the courage and endurance of people who managed to make a space for their children to live and grow happily when all around the world had gone quite mad.

Chapter 16: The Bogey Man

I was reared before the advent of child psychology. We were constantly threatened by our mother with a fate worse than death when we refused to do her bidding. If we strayed too far from home we were assured there were many creatures lying in wait to take children off with them, though my father always insisted if anyone took me by mistake they would return me post-haste.

Every child in the Faythe had heard the clip-clop of the headless horseman's horse as he patrolled the street late at night or the creak of the wheels of the carriage of death. We had nearly all caught glimpses of the pooka and heard the awful cry of the banshee in the dead of winter and watched the will-o'-the-wisp glowing at the back of Pat Molloy's field on foggy evenings. When we recited Yeats' poem calling the child away to the fairy place we took it as gospel because our mother often pointed out changelings to us, fairy men or women left in place of stolen human children, in fact she often hinted she was not too sure about me.

This was a time when even radio was a novelty and the rich folklore of Ireland had not been beaten into the Celtic mists by multi-channel television. My father and mother were natural storytellers like most of their generation. They were telling what they had been told and we drank in a rich mixture of religion laced with superstition and mythology, a hodge-podge of truth and fiction with very blurred dividing lines. Our fears were also blurred, we loved to dare the night just a little and the darkness, for all it contained, remained friendly, ever friendly.

On autumn evenings when our mothers came to the doors to round up the flock and we were reluctant to leave our games the threat was, "The Bogey Man will get you if you don't come in." The Bogey Man was one of the least offensive of our invisible foes and we took little or no notice of him. We were never too convinced of his malicious intent. I think we felt he could be easily won over to our side, or maybe it was that familiarity breeds contempt and the threat was used too often.

Just as surely as mothers know when a child's cry really signals disaster, we could read the tone of voice of our elders. We knew when our mother meant business and then we moved. So it was that one autumn there was a strange unease in our street. When we were called in we sensed a new urgency in the voices calling and we did not delay. There was a new edge to the darkness, a sharper cutting edge that we instinctively held back from. We were curious and wary and we kept our ears and eyes open for clues. It was obvious there was something afoot. We overheard snatches of conversation between adults and we caught their anxiety from them. In those days children were never really told anything, only issued with vague excuses; we could only make wild guesses as to what was at the heart of the matter.

When we asked outright we were told the Bogey Man was around the area and we must not go far from home or stay out after dark. This did not faze us too much until the awful day came when we were barred from Pat Molloy's field and the rocks at the back of our houses. We were to stay in our own yards, not even to venture to the end of our own gardens. This was too much. We might as well have been jailed we were so curtailed by these orders. How could we survive at all if the world at the back was forbidden to us? Certainly we could not obey these unreasonable commands, the rules of war were too severe, so we called a council meeting on the malt-house steps and my brother, who could always get round my mother, was delegated to find out what he could. Of course he had to pick his time, such matters were delicate and had to be handled carefully or the results could be disastrous and end in total failure.

While we waited for word from headquarters we pieced together what information we had between us. It was obvious, even to the youngest, that there was some new threat that the adults were taking very seriously.

This was not the old familiar Bogey Man of previous years, It was a new and more virulent strain which spelled trouble. He had been referred to by some people as the "Hairy Man" and he was sighted in the fields at the back of the Faythe. The descriptions were varied. Some swore he was a big hairy creature, as tall as eight or nine feet, with huge hands and feet. we had one report of a footprint, found in the bog under Maiden Tower which would make the Yeti look dainty.

Food had gone missing from kitchen windows, tarts put out to cool on sills disappeared, plate and all. Though none of us were above taking the odd bun or scone we knew no child would be daring enough to lift a whole apple tart, including the plate. Clothes also disappeared from the clothes-lines, shirts and even a work pants belonging to one man. We could not see how little Mr Browne's dungarees could be of any use to an eight-foot Bogey Man. He was only a shade over five feet and as thin as a stick. It was said that on windy days he had to fill his pockets with stones to keep from blowing away.

Rumour had it that his wife often carried him home in her large apron when he had too much to drink. I was told, on one occasion when accosted by the local garda and asked what she was carrying, her sizzled husband stuck his head out of her voluminous folded apron and said with dignity, "A man, be God."

In due course my brother came back from the front with the story. There was a dangerous creature on the loose, nobody knew what he, it, was but it certainly did exist somewhere in the vicinity and had even been written up in the "Free Press." The guards were searching the fields and rocks way out as far as the Rosslare Road and nobody was safe while this hairy bogey man roamed.

We had mixed feelings about this news. It certainly added a dash of excitement to our lives and we sat around discussing the mystery man for many enjoyable hours, but it also put a stop to our gallop and led us to being closely watched and supervised at all times, something we found most irksome. We could not decide if we were for or against our hairy visitor and longed for a glimpse of him or a trace even in the long grass. Of course we broke bounds and went in search of the foe and the bravest of us even broke curfew and stole out after dark hoping to be the one to bring back solid evidence.

The stories grew as the winter progressed and so did the stature and width of the creature. It was said that he killed one of Nick Kelly's cows, with his bare hands, and left nothing but the bones licked clean as evidence of his terrible meal. He could be heard wailing and roaring at night by all accounts his cry was louder than Tarzan's and more blood-curdling than the banshees. He was seen leaping from the top of Maiden Tower, the highest rock in the whole area, and standing astride Three Span, the gorge in the rocks where it is said Cromwell threw the people to their death when he captured the town.

As winter deepened and we could not get out to explore any more the mystery man paled into insignificance. We no longer cared if he roamed our patch because we were confined to base anyhow. Since he refused to show himself and the stories had become so outrageous, even the most gullible amongst us had become sceptical, we began to lose interest. We had other fish to fry. The Hairy Bogey Man of the Faythe slowly passed into legend and became one more tale to tell on winter evenings around the fire.

The truth when it emerged was ignored in favour of the more interesting fiction. Apparently the story behind the legend was that some poor fellow who deserted from the Irish Army was hiding out in a concrete hut, which was built in the rocks during the Emergency to hold a gun. He was eventually found by the guards and trundled back to face the music.

Chapter 17: Winter

When we look back to our youth our summers seem to have been made up of long lazy unending days of sunshine lasting forever. Winter meant short crisp days and long mellow evenings. How is it that now the reverse is true? Winter seems to last for nine months of cold damp misery and we wait anxiously for a glimpse of the sun during the summer months, afraid to miss that one fine day which could be all we get for the season. Ah, childhood, no wonder we hold on to it so fiercely and mourn its passing so vehemently.

Everyone has a store of memories hoarded away like precious possessions in a hand-carved box; a silk scarf to hold against the cheek, a lace handkerchief to touch, a brooch, a ring. On lonely days we can take them out for consolation. No matter how cerebral we become the instincts take over at times of greatest need and what carries us through is not words but times remembered. I try not to ponder infinity too much, I find it bad for my melancholic streak, but when I think of weighty matters like life after death, or the Creator of the Universe, I become convinced that God is the familiar. How else could we be expected to enjoy existing forever? The familiar is best conjured up for me by remembering the way I felt on a winter's evening, in the forties, when I was about four years old. I was taken down to the quay by a cousin of mine to see an American ship anchored there. As we turned the corner at the top of King Street, there it was, towering like a huge mountain, or so it seemed to me at the time. The day was cold but crisp and clear and I was being pushed in a tan-sad, a type of folding pram, well wrapped and wearing a fur bonnet and new fur mittens, so it must have been soon after Christmas or maybe early February after my birthday.

That day must have been the perfect blend of safety and adventure, wonder and contentment because my subconscious selected it from all the other days of my childhood, like someone selecting the best photograph to be enlarged and framed and kept forever. I remember the cold on my cheeks, the warmth of the fur gloves, the awesome sight we were looking at, something totally alien to my world and then, the return home. I sat in front of the glowing range in our room, my mother fed us scrambled eggs on toast and listened as I struggled to describe what I had seen. One of my first voyages into the unknown and now I was safe again. I had made the first tentative leap and everything I had left was still waiting for me, not diminished, nothing lost but something gained. That evening is etched on my memory forever. The familiar has many faces.

The sign that winter had really arrived in our house was not the early drawing of the curtains or the range glowing all day, but the fact that our boxes were pulled out from their hiding places, dusted off and delved into.

Last years paint-boxes, crayons and various games were inspected and the suspicion that our mother had done a little clearing out was very strong. The contents of the three large cardboard containers always looked neat and tidy, had always settled down too well below the level we had left them in spring. We soon set out our paraphernalia around the room. My brother's Meccano sets and dinky cars and my celluloid dolls and scraps of material vied with each other for space. My older brother had his schoolroom in the corner and proceeded to introduce me to the intricacies of algebra by chalking on the end of the wooden seat and I tried my best to be a willing pupil.

It must be true that memory is selective because even though we endured near Spartan-like conditions in our house, during winter, my memories are all of warmth and comfort and the luxury of a hot-water-bottle to toast my toes on extra-frosty nights. My father reading the paper, the clack-clack of my mother's knitting needles and my brothers and myself sitting at the big round table in the room, busy about our own pursuits – that's the picture I have of winter nights in the house in the Faythe.

Our most treasured possession was a wind-up gramophone and a pile of records we were forbidden to touch. John Boles singing "Song of the Dawn". Gene Autrey crooning "Springtime in the Rockies" and my own favourite Delia Murphy's version of "If I were a Blackbird" were among the collection. We loved to listen but not in the ordinary way. The minute our parents were out of the way we set to it with a will. We had discovered how to manipulate the machine which had to be wound up by hand. If we wound up madly we could increase the speed of the record and by letting it run down we could slow the singer to a drawl. Poor Delia Murphy's blackbird flew at the speed of light and Delia sounded like the modern day recording of the Chipmunks while John Bowles was usually given no revs at all and sounded like Chaliapin in slow motion.

When we had no energy left to turn the handle, or when we were tired listening to the singers' frantic efforts we made a sortie on the press at the back of the gramophone. There was another forbidden area where the gas masks were kept and the most daring thing we could possibly do was to prise open the door and remove the boxes with their gruesome contents. If the coast was clear we could go so far as to put the gas masks on our heads and trail around the room. We were too young to be frightened by thoughts of poisoned gas. I know the concept of war never really meant anything to me at all when I was a child.

Before we had a wireless of our own we would go to a neighbour's house to listen to Dick Barton Special Agent. Every evening we gathered to listen to the further adventures of Dick himself and his trusty sidekicks, Snowy and Jock. Every child on the street was glued to the wireless at the same time and when we met the next day we would act out the episode, with, of course, a few minor adjustments to the script. I remember the excitement when our house was at last wired for electricity and among other marvels we became the proud possessors of an electric kettle. Now we had our own wireless and the world really opened up to us. The first American influence came via AFN, the American Air Force Network, and "Sunday Night is Music Night" brought all the English Music Hall acts into our front room. Most of my generation became Goon fans when Spike Milligan and the boys created a whole new form of broadcasting and humour.

Like all the other seasons of my childhood, winter never seemed too long, or too cold, or too wet, it was just right. Now and then we ventured out of doors when cabin fever threatened. The wind, whistling down the Faythe, made it impossible to dawdle around doors and to sit on cold cement steps would be courting disaster.

Trapped under mountains of wool our adventures were seriously curtailed and the best we could hope for was a heavy frost or a fall of snow. When the frost glistened on the paths we made slides. Some of us even smuggled out buckets of water under cover of darkness. Throwing it on the paths helped nature along and ensured a good glassy surface next day. Threats of every form of punishment short of torture and death by the adult population of the street, who were terrified to walk outside their front doors, let alone risk the perilous descent of Castle Hill Street on frosty mornings, did nothing to stop the budding Sonja Henies on the street.

We slid on regardless and I suppose the lack of broken bones was due more to the padding our heavy winter clothes gave us, than to our skill at keeping our balance on the glassy paths and streets.

I remember one winter, I think it was after the hot summer of nineteen-forty-seven, when we awoke one morning to a white world. The snow had fallen steadily during the night and continued all next day. We gazed in wonder, with our noses pressed against the freezing window panes and watched our street disappear under a blanket of white that lay undisturbed by a footprint or a mark of any sort. From the upstairs windows, as far as the eye could see, a vast trackless white land was spread out, a little frightening in its unfamiliarity. When the snow stopped falling and the frost set in towards evening, lights began to appear around Pat Molloy's field and dark figures could be seen heading in the general direction of Hilly Holly, a huge hill field under the rocks. The ever resourceful people of the Faythe and the surrounding streets were not going to let the opportunity for a little winter sport pass them by. The excitement was contagious and soon most of the population of the town seemed to be gathered on the snowy slopes, sliding on everything from tin trays and sheets of galvanise to hastily-made toboggans and it looked as if all our Christmas cards had come to life.

The snow lasted for nearly a week and this time even the adults were sorry when the thaw set in and our fields returned to their normal winter colours.

I suppose we were the last generation to sit around the fire on winter nights when people had to make their own enjoyment and when company was precious and storytelling an art. We children were expert at coaxing the older people to talk about their youth and tell the yarns that we knew nearly by heart but never tired of hearing. We were convinced for years that my father could speak German and a smattering of what he called bog-Latin. He had a nice tenor voice and when he had given the favourites like "There's a little Green Road winding over the Hill" or reduced us to surreptitious tears with "The Little Toy Soldier" he would even things out with a spirited rendition of "Lili Marlene" in English, German and bog-Latin.

The question, "Do you believe in ghosts?" was sure to get things going and we could settle back for an hour or two after throwing that one into the company at large. My mother was streets ahead of everyone else in this department, probably because she had just one story and it never failed to raise goosebumps on her listeners. Unlike my father who was given to flights of fancy and liked to embellish his yarns a bit too much, her story delivered in matter-of-fact tones was totally believable. She always began by insisting she did not expect to be believed, she had no explanation for what happened one night when she was first married and living in a little house in Lower King Street. My father was away all night working at the Pier Head and she was alone in the house with a very young baby at the time. She was awakened from a deep sleep by a terrible wailing sound that made her hair stand on end and brought a cold sweat out on her back. At this point in the narrative she would pause for effect and look at each one of us to see if she was getting the desired reaction. Satisfied. she would continue. She knew that a poor woman was in the habit of passing down the street at night with a child in a pram and she thought to herself that was what the noise was, but she was not convinced. Never one to back away from anything, she got out of bed and went to the window, but the street was empty and the terrible wailing went on.

It was her description of the deserted street, the unearthly noise and her own fear that made the story so gripping and we always sat rooted to the spot waiting for the climax even though we knew it verbatim. Next day my mother discovered that her neighbours' young daughter had died during the night at the very hour when she had heard the terrible keening of the banshee.

Making our way to bed after a night of such stories we did not trust the darkness on our own hall or stairs and every squeak sounded menacing. The relief of reaching the bed and pulling the eiderdown over our heads was exquisite. As we lay quaking in the soft blackness we resolved to listen to no more stories, a resolution we knew in our hearts we could not keep.

Chapter 18: Cures

There is nothing new under the sun. When I hear people talking today about alternative medicine and natural cures I remember all the journeys we made as children to people with the "cure" and all the obnoxious concoctions we swallowed in the name of health. Every child of my generation has a natural aversion to herbal tea. Who can forget the sickly potion of senna leaves brewed every week and presented with dire threats of everything from headaches to internal combustion to be visited on us if we did not swallow it to the bitter dregs? And bitter they were, second only to the terrible cocktail of sulphur and molasses we had to down at the onset of spring to clear the blood and the complexion at the same time.

Doctors were rarely seen in our street and if one was called it was certainly a case of grave necessity. Most babies were born at home with the local midwife in attendance and there were women in every community who were on hand at times of sickness and calamity.

Some of them were better than both doctors and nurses.

One of my aunts was such a woman. My mother's older sister was a big woman with piercing blue eyes and a steady calm presence who seemed to appear whenever there was a sickness or trouble of any sort in our house.

These women washed the newborn babies and laid them in their mothers' arms and they were there to wash the bodies of the dead and lay them in their coffins. They were made by the needs of the society they lived in and were made redundant by the evolution of the same society into a money-making machine. Now they are few and far between and are looked on as a sort of phenomenon. Maybe as people become more and more disillusioned with the abuse of medicine and drugs in the present day they will emerge again to point the way to a saner and more caring way to live and stay healthy.

At the top of our street lived a woman who had a cure for worms. This was one of the afflictions which seemed to be prevalent among children when I was young and many children were struck down with something called worm fever. I never delved into this particular malady but I remember my local GP backing off in horror when my mother taxed him in the Sixties, when he arrived to treat one of my own ailing children, in our house in Dublin. "Would you not think," says she, "that the child might have worms?" I can't for the life of me remember what his answer was, but I can still see his face and the haste with which he made his retreat.

My mother swore worms were caught by eating clay, so babies, who have a natural inclination to put everything into their mouths regardless, had to be watched carefully at all times to make sure they were not engaged in this dodgy exercise.

If anyone displayed symptoms that did not respond to the usual dosages they were marched up for the worm cure every week. We were convinced the old lady who dispensed the salty liquid was a witch. She was a very old woman of dark complexion, probably due to poring over her potions and lotions, and she went through a strange ritual, part religion, part magic. The child on the receiving end had to kneel in front of the ancient crone who anointed the head and the hands three times in the name of the Father, Son and the Holy Ghost, and then three sips of the brew had to be swallowed again in the name of the Trinity. This ritual was performed every day for nine days without fail to make sure the cure worked and if a day was missed the whole process had to begin again from scratch.

At one time some of my friends were taking the cure so I managed to persuade the powers that be that I needed to accompany them. I paraded up for the nine days just to see what went on behind the closed doors.

There was a long queue each evening. The boys pushing and jostling, the girls trying to look nonchalant.

All of us proud to bear the stigma and hoping the cure would leave a mark on our foreheads that might possibly be of some use in currying favours or help us dodge some homework. We approached the inner sanctum one by one and knelt to be anointed. I still remember the salty taste of the potion itself. I think I gave up after a few days when I became bored with the whole thing and took a walk up the Rocks Lane instead.

Never an over-robust child, I was always falling prey to one sickness or another. I used to go to another "healer" on the back of my father's bicycle. This man was a friend of his who lived in Ferrycarrig. I loved those journeys through the still summer evenings and I felt a bit like a swan skimming along the Slaney as my father cycled smoothly towards Lady Dane's, with me strapped into a special seat on the back and nothing separating me from the still waters of the river but the tall grasses and reeds beside the road.

We would stop at the little wall before we came to the Demesne and take a drink of water from the pump on the side of the road. My father would point out the various trees and name the different bird-calls sounding in the air above our heads. There was never a car to disturb the tranquil evening and hardly even another soul to be seen once we passed the walkers at the out-skirts of the town. My father would speak at great length about the man we were visiting who could cure so many things, even stop the flow of blood from a wound. I have only the vaguest recollection of the man and his daughter to whom he passed on the cures. The important thing for me was the journey. I suppose I could be accused of malingering, I loved these voyages with my father so much.

We are told in the Scripture that a woman forgets the pains of labour when her child is born into the world. I was a bit sceptical of this particular passage before my children were born and even for a long time afterwards.

But as time went by I realised. the truth of the matter.

Not just the pains of childbirth but all pain fades and is forgotten and we only remember the good bits. Looking back over my life I find it hard to remember the bad times and my childhood, especially, is painted with definite tinges of rose.

Think of Picasso, looking, I always thought, like a particularly wrinkled infant in his later years, striving to capture in his work an innocence and simplicity, once given, now lost. Leaving everything learned aside and yet using it to find his way, he succeeded in producing something that grabs at the heart and makes us vibrate to the core of our beings with half-remembered feelings we cannot name.

Having passed the half-century, a strong sense of this simplifying process is taking over. My life becomes less complicated as I throw away most of the accumulated clutter. As this automatic clearance takes place I find some of the savour and zest I thought I had lost, or left way back there, returning. Time is not my master now, I am gaining the upper hand. My days for the most part are delightfully unstructured and stretch out in an unknown and exciting path before me. The struggle, and in my case, open war, of growing and knowing has lost its cutting edge and I find each day becoming quite the adventure it used to be when I was young. I am privileged to live in the country in neat-isolation, in a cottage and surroundings that understand me well. I have become convinced that the cure for life is living.

This open secret we lose sight of as we hurry to leave childhood behind us. Wasn't it Shaw who said, "Youth is such a precious thing it should never be given to the young"? The truth is, it is never taken away, it just lies dormant until we get sense enough to take it up again.

I have a friend who refers to his thirty-odd years of marriage as "The great survival." I like to think of my fifty-odd years of living as a great survival, too, and when I look forward I remember one of my mother's sayings. A woman who certainly took "the cure" she lived life to the very best of her ability. When throwing caution to the wind and deciding to go for something without worrying about the consequence she would say:

"When it is a day, let it be a day.

Give us another Ha'pert of Goosegobs."

When our mother said this we knew we were in for a good time, whatever the cost.

What the Green Rushes Whisper

by Vonnie Banville Evans

This is a novel about a time when history was about to explode. It is set in a period just before the Great War, before the Easter Rising, before the War of Independence and leading up to the 1913 Lockout in Ireland. Big Jim Larkin, James Connolly and Richard Corish were striding the streets of Wexford.

It is a story of an ordinary woman and her life. It is a story of service and courage.

Vonnie Banville Evans draws upon her own Grandmother's life and the history of her home town. She reflects the language, beliefs and hopes of the people of that time. She writes with great sympathy for all those living in the shadow of tumultuous change.

Anna's Dream

by Vonnie Banville Evans

"The rocks which rise behind Anna Dunville's house in Wexford are the gathering place for her gang of friends, where they build huts and plan adventures. But no adventure could match the one that awaits Anna in Vonnie Banville Evans' Anna's Dream...a gripping story that leads Anna and her friends to delve into the terrible events of three hundred years before, when Cromwell and his troops laid waste to the town."

Gordon Snell - The Irish Times

Also from Code Green Publishing:

The Trousers *of* Reality

"We all need this book. Read it, listen to it, let it speak to you. It can change your life for the better."
From the foreword Wyatt Woodsmall PH.D.
Co-founder of the International NLP Trainers Association

Art, philosophy, psychology, history, science, music and DIY are explored in a search for principles that work. It shows you how to discover why they work and how to apply all of the skills you might have however you came by them.

This book is for you if you would like to understand how to make best use of all of the resources available to you. It is aimed at those who see life, both work and play, as an amazing opportunity to achieve excellence and find meaning in every breath.

www.TrousersOfReality.com